The
DOG EXPERT

Karen Bush

Project Consultant: Dr. D. G. Hessayon

Published by Expert Books
a division of Transworld Publishers

Copyright © Karen Bush and Dr. D. G. Hessayon 2010

The right of Karen Bush to be identified as author of this work
and Dr. D. G. Hessayon as Project Consultant for the work has been asserted
in accordance with sections 77 and 78 of the Copyright Designs and Patents Act 1988.

Illustrations copyright © Claire Colvin 2010

A catalogue record for this book is available from the British Library

TRANSWORLD PUBLISHERS
61-63 Uxbridge Road, London W5 5SA
a division of the Random House Group Ltd

 Distributed in the United States
by Sterling Publishing Co. Inc.,
387 Park Avenue South,
New York,
NY 10016-8810

EXPERT BOOKS

CONTENTS

The Random House Group Ltd supports the Forest Stewardship Council (FSC), the leading International forest-certification organization. All our titles that are printed on Greenpeace approved FSC-certified paper carry the FSC logo. Our paper procurement policy can be found at www.rbooks.co.uk/environment

Reproduction by Spot On Digital Imaging Ltd, Gomm Road, High Wycombe, Bucks HP13 7DJ
Printed and bound in Great Britain by Butler, Tanner & Dennis Ltd, Frome

Designed by Robert Updegraff

Printed and bound by Butler Tanner & Dennis Ltd, Frome, Somerset

ISBN 978 0903505 7 1 0

© Karen Bush and Dr. D. G. Hessayon 2011

FSC

MIX
Paper from responsible sources
FSC® C023561

Chapter 1

YOU AND YOUR DOG

Dogs can be wonderful companions, giving tremendous pleasure, entertainment and affection, but they are also a big responsibility. They can be demanding in terms of both time and money, and when you acquire one you'll be committing yourself to caring for him* for 10–15 years, or possibly longer.

Becoming a dog owner is not a decision to take lightly: before making it you should carefully examine your reasons for wanting a dog and ensure that right from the start you have a very clear idea of what will be involved.

If you are still certain that it's the right thing to do, be prepared to spend plenty of time researching what sort of dog will be best for you. Making the wrong choice – or the wrong decision to have a dog in the first place – can have tragic consequences if you then find that you are unable to keep him. It is estimated that around 20,000 dogs in the UK and 2–3 million in the US are destroyed each year for lack of a home. If you aren't sure whether you have what it takes to be a good dog owner, then offer to help as a volunteer at a local rescue centre to find out if this is going to be the right pet for you.

* The dog in the text throughout this book is referred to as 'him', but the words apply equally to females.

Why do you want a dog?

This is the first question to ask yourself, and for most people there is a whole variety of reasons rather than one single answer. Dogs are fun to have around; they encourage you to take more exercise; and when you're out together they can be great ice-breakers, helping you make new friends, while at home you can spend time playing or simply relaxing and enjoying each other's company.

However, if the main reason is to make you feel safer, then get an efficient alarm system instead. Buying a dog to provide someone to pour your heart out to or to boost your self-esteem may be a comfort to you, but using a dog as an emotional crutch won't necessarily help you and may lead to behaviour problems in him. Neither should you fall into the trap of getting a dog simply because he looks cute or is fashionable. You need to do thorough research beforehand and be prepared to treat him like a dog, not an accessory.

Can you afford a dog?

Before you even get your dog, you may find yourself spending money in order to make your home dog-friendly and escape-proof. After this you'll need to buy all the necessities in readiness for his arrival (see pages 46–47) and prepare your house and garden (see pages 48–51).

Then there's his initial purchase price (which could be anything from around £100 to £2,000 or even more), followed by regular outgoings on food, insurance and preventative health care, plus any incidental veterinary bills, holiday care and extras you might like to buy, such as treats, toys and replacing damaged or outgrown equipment. Anticipate spending somewhere in the region of £1,000–£1,500 a year every year for a small to medium-sized dog, and considerably more if you choose a large or giant breed.

Do you have enough time for a dog?

A relationship with a dog is a very interactive one, and you should expect to put as much into it as you get out. As well as ensuring your dog has sufficient exercise, you'll need to be prepared to spend time training, grooming and playing with him every day. If you want to come home after work and just put your feet up, you should consider a less demanding pet.

If you have to work long hours, get a pet who will require less attention than a dog.

What hours do you work?

If you're out at work all day it won't be fair to get a puppy or youngster, who may become bored, miserable, lonely and likely to develop behaviour problems as a result (see Chapter 6). Provided you don't work excessively long hours and if you think carefully about your choice, having a full-time job need not necessarily be a bar to owning a dog. Retired greyhounds and many older dogs in rescue still have much to offer and will be happy to doze while you are out.

Four hours is the maximum length of time your dog should be left alone, though, and if you can't manage to get home at lunchtimes to see to him, you'll need to make other arrangements. 'Doggy daycare' centres are becoming more common, or you could ask a friend, relative or dog-walker to come and take him out to relieve himself and to spend a little time interacting with him.

Where do you live?

On the whole, dogs are very adaptable, but it's important to choose the right breed for the place you live. Large breeds may feel cramped and may be constantly underfoot if your home is small, for example. If you live in rented accommodation you should check whether there are any restrictions on keeping pets. Location can also be important, as although many breeds will be quite at home in cities and towns, others require a more rural environment that allows greater opportunity for free-running exercise.

Who shares your home?

Think carefully about getting a dog if others who share your home aren't as enthusiastic about it as you; going ahead regardless can lead to friction and resentments, and even to spitefulness towards the pet, all of which may lead to behaviour problems (see Chapter 6).

If you have children, most will be thrilled by the prospect of getting a dog, and they will learn a lot about life, responsibility and respect for living creatures from having one around; but don't allow them to pressure you into making such a decision unless you are 100 per cent committed to the idea yourself. You will ultimately be responsible for the dog's daily care, and your active involvement will increase if the children lose interest once the novelty wears off, or when they go to college, university or leave home.

Do you have other pets?

You also need to consider any other pets you may own. Some older dogs may get a new lease of life from having a youngster around, but others may find the newcomer a nuisance and become snappy and irritable unless interaction between the two is carefully monitored and the older dog given some respite when he needs it.

If you have a dog with a behaviour problem, don't get a second in an attempt to help solve it, as you are just as likely to end up with two dogs with the same problem.

Some dogs will happily accept cats, rabbits, guinea pigs, hamsters and other small furry pets, but they will need careful introductions and supervision when they are together. Other dogs may have a very high chase drive and will never be safe to keep with such pets. Equally, some cats will never feel comfortable with a dog around, no matter how well behaved the dog may be.

Choosing the right breed, age and sex of dog will be essential if you have other pets, but before even getting to that point, you need to think very carefully about the effect he is likely to have and whether getting a dog will be fair on them.

Are you willing to make a few sacrifices?

Taking on a dog may mean it will be necessary for you to make a few compromises in your lifestyle:

- You'll need to go straight home after work, rather than out with colleagues.
- You may need to get up earlier in order to take your dog out.
- You may have to take more exercise than you are accustomed to.
- When you want to go on holiday, or even for a day out, you will need to plan ahead.

What are your future plans?

No matter how much you may be looking forward to getting a dog, postpone it if any predictable major changes or upheavals in life are looming, such as marriage, divorce, house move, pregnancy, large family celebrations, an imminent holiday, or if you are experiencing a period of bereavement. It is stressful enough for any dog, whether puppy or adult, to come into a new home without having to cope with all the extra disturbance caused by such events; and it will also make it difficult for you to concentrate on his needs.

You will need to consider whether a dog will be compatible with other pets you may own.

QUESTIONS ABOUT YOUR DOG

Dogs come in all shapes and sizes and with different characteristics – decide which ones you like and those you really couldn't live with. It's vitally important to be honest, as developing a good bond depends on finding the dog most compatible with your own likes, dislikes and temperament. Remember to take into account other members of your household too, as this will also be a factor affecting your choice of dog.

Big or small?

Smaller dogs generally tend to live longer than larger ones and eat less, so will be cheaper to feed, and they take up less space in your home.

A bigger dog won't necessarily need more exercise than a small or medium-sized one. It varies from breed to breed, but some big dogs can be quite low-maintenance in this respect. You will however need sufficient space in your home, and his strength and bulk may be a problem for young or frail members of the household. Although big dogs don't live as long as their smaller relatives, they usually take longer to reach maturity.

Active or couch potato?

All dogs will need exercise every day, but the amount and type can differ considerably. If you are a keen walker, plan to jog with your dog or to take up a sport such as cani-cross, then it makes sense to choose a breed that will be able to cope. If you're not a great fan of exercise, however, don't pick a high-activity breed, as failure to provide an adequate outlet for all that energy will result in a frustrated dog likely to resort to destructive or other behaviour problems (see Chapter 6). A very boisterous dog – especially if he is large or muscular in build – may also be an unsuitable choice if you have small children or frail elderly relatives sharing your house.

How much grooming do you want to do?

Steer clear of breeds with high-maintenance coats unless you're prepared to put in quite a bit of work every day. Some people love spending time on grooming, but it's not everyone's cup of tea and, if not properly cared for, some coats can quickly form uncomfortable matts and knots. Clipping can be an alternative option if you don't intend to show your dog, but his coat will still need regular, if less time-consuming, attention between clips.

Trainability

Unless you have lots of experience, it is advisable to choose a breed that is relatively easy to train rather than one that is inclined to be independent and strong-willed. Training should be an ongoing process and should be continued even after basic obedience has been established. With an intelligent dog who requires plenty of mental stimulation, you may need to be prepared to put in extra effort thinking up different ways to provide him with new challenges.

There's a size and type of dog to suit everyone. Be realistic about which will be the best match for you.

Two dogs can be good company for each other, but will also be twice the work and expense for you.

How houseproud are you?

If you're particularly houseproud or a fanatical gardener, then a dog probably isn't the pet for you. Whichever breed you choose, you'll need to be prepared for a certain amount of mess, but some are more inclined than others to slobber, moult, dig, soak up vast quantities of water in their coats or acquire acres of mud in their paws. Choose a breed that will be able to fit in comfortably with your domestic preferences.

One dog or two?

Two dogs can help each other exercise by playing together out of doors, and they'll have each other for company when you have to go out. The downside is that two will mean twice the work for you, as well as double the expense, because you will need to spend time training and interacting with them individually as well as together so that they do not become closer to each other than to you.

If, however, you are sure you would like to have two dogs, wait until your first one is at least a year old and both basic obedience and a good bond with you have been established before getting a second one.

What will you want to do with your dog?

If you have in mind certain activities that you'd like to do with your dog, make sure you choose one that is going to suit your interests. If you want to do obedience work (see page 98), for example, pick a breed that thrives on learning and likes to please; or if you are keen on agility, select one that has the necessary athleticism and the right disposition.

Pick a breed which is likely to fit in with your interests and lifestyle.

Remember that little puppies can grow into large adults. Make sure you know, as far as you are able, what you are taking on.

Puppy or adult?

Puppies are cute, but they're also hard work, can be very time-consuming, and will need special attention while they're growing up. Although an adolescent or adult dog will still require time, effort and commitment, this may sometimes be an easier option. Think carefully about which is right for you.

PUPPY

Advantages

- Puppies are cute and appealing, and it's usually very easy for the two of you to bond with each other.
- You're starting with a clean slate, and can help develop his character and behaviour in the way you want.
- You will have the pleasure of watching your puppy growing up.
- If you have other pets, it may be easier for you to teach him how to behave around them. His age may also make them feel less threatened, so it might be easier for them to accept him than to accept an older dog.

Disadvantages

- You'll need to be at home for a large part of the day while your puppy is growing up. Like a young child, he'll require close supervision, will need feeding several times a day at first, and will need to go out frequently to relieve himself.
- Puppies can be quite destructive and inclined to chew while young.
- You will need to put a lot of work into socializing him while he is young so that he doesn't develop fears and phobias as an adult.

ADULT

Advantages

- An adult dog won't need constant supervision and is less likely to chew or be destructive.
- He may be house-trained and may already have received basic obedience training.
- You will still be able to look forward to many years together without all the hassle of raising a puppy.
- If he's a mixed-breed dog of unknown parentage, you'll see immediately what his full size is – with a puppy all you can do is guess.

Disadvantages

- Depending on where you get him, you may know little or nothing about your dog's previous history, and he may have emotional and behaviour problems that need to be worked through.
- An older dog may be more set in his ways. Although it may take a little more time and patience, even old dogs can learn new tricks, so this needn't be a major disadvantage.
- If he is an adolescent, you may still find your hands full, as they can be very boisterous and enthusiastic. They are often handed in for rehoming because they have grown out of the cute puppy stage and the owner hasn't anticipated or been able to cope with the adolescent phase.

Elderly dogs

Don't dismiss the idea of a more elderly 'senior' dog. Quieter, more settled and less demanding in terms of exercise, he will be just as able to form a close relationship with you as a younger model. Often overlooked in rescue shelters, a golden oldie can still have plenty of years ahead, will repay you tenfold in terms of affection and company, and can make a great pet if you are unable to cope with the demands of caring for a puppy or adolescent.

Male or female?

You may have a definite preference, but if not, choose the individual you like best, regardless of sex. The following differences are only generalizations, and there are always exceptions.

FEMALES

- Often said to be more affectionate and sensitive than males.
- May be easier to train.
- Usually smaller in height and build than males.
- Unless neutered, will come into season twice a year.

MALES

- Inclined to be more independent, but more consistent in temperament than females.
- More likely to be territorial.
- Usually taller and more muscular in build than females.
- More likely to roam and to pick fights with other dogs, although neutering will lessen this tendency.

Mix'n'match

Both males and females can – and in the majority of cases do – live quite happily with other dogs of the same sex, but if you already have a resident canine and are planning on getting another, the safest choice is usually to pick one of the opposite sex. Two males is the next combination most likely to be successful. Many females get on amicably enough, but if they do fall out it can sometimes be on a spectacular scale and with major consequences. If you end up with a mixed-sex household, remember that neutering will be essential if you are to avoid an unwanted pregnancy.

SHOULD I NEUTER MY DOG?

Neutering is the removal of the sexual organs to prevent unplanned pregnancies and gender-related problems, such as females coming into season and males being inclined to stray or get into fights. It also eliminates the tremendous sexual frustration felt by both males and females when they are unable to get to each other and which can make them very stressed. Most dogs in rescue shelters are either neutered before being rehomed, or it is made one of the conditions of adoption that the new owner will arrange for this to be done.

If you want to breed from your dog, neutering is obviously not an option, but for most pets it makes them happier and easier to live with. Neutered dogs are more likely to gain weight, so you may need to reduce calorie intake slightly, but neutering won't have a large effect on personality. If anything, you may find your dog more attentive, relaxed and affectionate when no longer at the mercy of hormonally dictated behaviour. For more information on neutering, see page 111.

Neutering will not only prevent unplanned pregnancies but can also have health benefits.

Pedigree or crossbreed?

A pedigree is a pure-bred dog whose parents are both of the same breed, as are all their ancestors, traceable back to the establishment of their breed.

Although the terms are often used interchangeably, a crossbreed is the offspring of parents of two different pure breeds, while a mongrel is the result of random breeding, with one or both parents being of mixed ancestry.

Which you pick is down to personal preference – you may find yourself drawn to a particular breed, or you may prefer the unique individual looks of a mongrel or crossbreed. Whether pure-bred or of mixed ancestry, however, all dogs have one thing in common: running costs will be similar for both, with the exception of insurance, which can sometimes be more expensive for pedigrees.

PEDIGREES

- Have recognized breed characteristics, so it can be easier to pick the one that will best suit you in terms of size, weight, feeding, activity level, coat care and ease of training.
- Can be subject to certain hereditary and congenital disorders, although screening the parents for conditions for which testing is available can help minimize the chances of buying a puppy with a problem.
- Tend to be more expensive to buy than dogs of unknown parentage.

MONGRELS AND CROSSBREEDS

- Unless the parentage is known, it may be hard to predict what characteristics a puppy will exhibit as an adult dog.
- The more mixed the background, the more likely it is that the dog will benefit from 'hybrid vigour'. Although there is no guarantee that he will not be affected by inherited problems, the likelihood is reduced as his genes are drawn from a wider pool.
- Usually cheaper to buy than pedigrees, although unlikely to be free even from a rescue organization. The exceptions are the popular 'designer' dogs such as 'Labradoodles' (Labrador x Poodle) and 'Puggles' (Pug x Beagle) which, although technically crossbreeds, can be more expensive to buy than their pedigree parents.

Pedigrees have certain predictable characteristics.

Mongrels are unique 'one-offs' and can have much to offer.

RESEARCHING BREEDS

Although looks may be part of what initially attracts you to a certain breed, don't just fall for a pretty face, quirky look or a dog that appeals to your ego or the image you want to project. You need to be realistic about the type of dog you can take on and whether you will be compatible with each other. This means spending time thoroughly researching those breeds in which you are interested. Don't just find out about the positive points – ensure you are familiar with any less

favourable ones too and also with any health issues known to affect the breed.

Discover more by reading breed-specific books, articles in magazines and on the internet. Contact breed clubs, and talk to breeders, other owners and to instructors at dog training clubs. Attending breed shows will also help fill in any gaps in your knowledge. In the UK the Discover Dogs Show, held twice yearly, provides another opportunity to meet breeds you like and to learn more about them.

BREED GROUPS

Although these days the majority of dogs are kept as pets rather than as working animals, it is essential to consider what job the breed originally did, as specifically bred-for traits will dictate behaviour and activity levels.

All the breeds are categorized according to the purposes for which they were once used, and if you aren't sure what breed you'd like, then looking for breed-group characteristics that will fit in with the lifestyle and environment you can offer may be a good starting point.

■ GUNDOG

An affable temperament and a happy, fun-loving attitude to life, plus generally being easy to train, mean that many of the breeds in this group are popular as family pets. Intelligent and enthusiastic, their high energy levels do mean they will need plenty of exercise. They can make good pets for active first-time owners and families with sufficient home and garden space.

Examples: Cocker Spaniel, English Setter, English Springer Spaniel, Golden Retriever, Labrador Retriever.

■ HOUND

This group contains breeds originally used for hunting either by scent or sight. Generally laid back, they can make good companions, but may also possess an independent streak. As hounds are easily diverted by sight or scent, plenty of work will need to be put into achieving a good recall (see page 91). It may be possible to train them to live with small furry pets in your home, but they may never be reliable with other people's pets. Room for free-running exercise will be needed.

Try to find a dog which matches your lifestyle.

Examples: Basset Hound, Beagle, Dachshund, Greyhound, Whippet.

■ PASTORAL

This group contains the herding breeds – agile and active with high energy levels, these are the workaholics of the dog world and they'll generally take as much exercise and mental stimulation as you can provide. You will need a garden as well as access to areas where they can run free. Many also have high-maintenance coats. Ideal only for active owners interested in training and activities such as agility or flyball to help occupy mind and body.

Examples: Border Collie, German Shepherd, Shetland Sheepdog, Welsh Corgi.

■ The colour shown against each breed group is used in the following pages to identify breeds belonging to this group.

■ TERRIER

Active and tough, terriers have been used for hunting vermin above and below ground since ancient times, so may retain a strong inclination to dig and to chase small furry animals. Big personalities, sometimes stubborn and independent, they're always on the go and need adequate opportunity for exercise. Plenty of socialization with other dogs will be needed when young and, as some can lack patience with youngsters, they are best suited to adults or families with older children.

Examples: Airedale Terrier, Border Terrier, Bull Terrier, Jack Russell Terrier, West Highland White Terrier.

■ TOY

Generally attention-loving and friendly, most of the dogs in this group were bred specifically as companions, although some are included due to their size. Although needing less exercise than other groups, they can nevertheless be quite active and most are also highly trainable. They can make good first-time pets, although the tinier, more delicately built breeds may be too fragile for boisterous families with young children.

Examples: Cavalier King Charles Spaniel, Chihuahua, Pekingese, Pug, Yorkshire Terrier.

■ UTILITY

This is a miscellaneous collection of those dogs bred to fulfil particular roles, but which don't really fit into any of the other groups. It contains breeds as diverse as the Dalmatian, bred to run behind horse-drawn carriages and guard possessions in them, and the Schipperke, used as ratters and guard dogs on canal barges.

Examples: Bulldog, Dalmatian, Miniature Schnauzer, Shih Tzu, Standard Poodle.

■ WORKING

This group contains dogs bred for very specific purposes, such as guarding, protection, herding, pulling loads, and search and rescue. They are highly trainable, but most are large, powerfully built dogs and generally suited to more experienced rather than first-time owners.

Examples: Bernese Mountain Dog, Dobermann, Great Dane, Mastiff, Rottweiler.

GUIDE TO BREEDS

With more than 400 different dog breeds, it would be impossible to include them all, so just 45 of the most popular are briefly described here. An average range of sizes and weights has been quoted, which may differ from those of the breed standard. If you wish to show your dog, you should consult the breed standard (available from the appropriate breed club) to check that he meets specific height/weight requirements. NB a dog's height is measured to his withers (the top of his shoulder).

■ AIREDALE TERRIER

Height: 56–61 cm
Weight: 20–23 kg
Average lifespan: 12–13 years
Temperament: Outgoing, courageous and intelligent.
Grooming: 🐾 🐾
Feeding: 🐾 🐾 🐾
Exercise: 🐾 🐾 🐾 🐾
Notes: Loyal, curious and with a big sense of humour, this is a real live-wire who loves to dig and thrives on company. Coat will need stripping (see page 65) or clipping two or three times a year, as well as daily grooming.

■ BASSET HOUND

Height: 33–38 cm
Weight: 18–27 kg
Average lifespan: 10–12 years
Temperament: Placid, affectionate and sweet natured.
Grooming: 🐾
Feeding: 🐾 🐾 🐾
Exercise: 🐾 🐾 🐾
Notes: Possesses strong pack instinct and will be unhappy if left alone for extended periods. Stubborn on occasion and single-minded when on the scent of prey.

Key: Each breed profile has been given a rating, up to a maximum of five, for level of grooming, amount of food required and the need for exercise (e.g. 🐾 🐾 🐾).

The group to which each breed belongs is indicated by the following colours:

■ **Gundog**   ■ **Toy**
  Hound   ■ **Utility**
■ **Pastoral**   ■ **Working**
■ **Terrier** .

■ BEAGLE

Height: 33–40 cm
Weight: 8–14 kg
Average lifespan: 12–14 years
Temperament: Amiable, alert and mischievous.
Grooming: 🐾
Feeding: 🐾 🐾 🐾 🐾
Exercise: 🐾 🐾 🐾 🐾
Notes: Tough and energetic, loves company and is good with children, but can be wilful. Has a strong hunting instinct and can be a consummate escape artist.

■ BERNESE MOUNTAIN DOG

Height: 58–70 cm
Weight: 38–41 kg
Average lifespan: 6–8 years
Temperament: Self-confident, good natured, friendly and fearless.
Grooming: 🐾 🐾 🐾
Feeding: 🐾 🐾 🐾 🐾
Exercise: 🐾 🐾 🐾 🐾
Notes: Sturdy, kind and devoted family dog who likes to be included in all activities. Needs good socialization and training, as guarding instinct may lead him to defend owner and property with determination.

■ BICHON FRISE

Height: 23–28 cm
Weight: 3–5.5 kg
Average lifespan: 13–14 years
Temperament: Gentle, playful, intelligent and companionable.
Grooming: 🐾 🐾 🐾
Feeding: 🐾
Exercise: 🐾 🐾
Notes: Thrives on attention, and can become destructive if left alone for long periods. Sometimes strong-willed and stubborn.

◼ BORDER COLLIE

Height: 46–53 cm
Weight: 14–22 kg
Average lifespan: 12–14 years
Temperament: Keen, alert, active and highly intelligent.
Grooming: 🐾🐾🐾
Feeding: 🐾🐾🐾🐾
Exercise: 🐾🐾🐾🐾🐾🐾

Notes: Excels in competitions such as flyball, agility, heelwork to music and obedience, which help satisfy both physical and psychological needs. Insufficient exercise and mental stimulation likely to lead to behaviour problems – a breed requiring great commitment from the owner.

◼ BORDER TERRIER

Height: 25–28 cm
Weight: 3–5.5 kg
Average lifespan: 13–15 years
Temperament: Full of fun and mischief, affectionate and even-tempered.
Grooming: 🐾
Feeding: 🐾🐾
Exercise: 🐾🐾🐾🐾

Notes: A small but very active breed which can be independent. Likes to dig and may be inclined to chase small animals. The coat will need stripping (see page 65) twice a year.

◼ BOSTON TERRIER

Height: 38–43 cm
Weight: 4.5–11.5 kg
Average lifespan: 14–16 years
Temperament: Lively, intelligent and full of fun.
Grooming: 🐾
Feeding: 🐾🐾
Exercise: 🐾🐾

Notes: A good-tempered, affectionate, entertaining, gentle and playful companion. He can also be determined and strong-willed – but quick to learn if it suits him.

◼ BOXER

Height: 53–63 cm
Weight: 25–32 kg
Average lifespan: 9–12 years
Temperament: Cheerful, playful and exuberant.
Grooming: 🐾
Feeding: 🐾🐾🐾🐾
Exercise: 🐾🐾🐾🐾

Notes: A great capacity for learning is sometimes accompanied by a stubborn streak. Boisterous enthusiasm combined with a powerful muscular physique may be too much for toddlers or frail seniors to cope with.

◼ BULLDOG

Height: 30–36 cm
Weight: 22–25 kg
Average lifespan: 8–12 years
Temperament: Affectionate, placid, determined and loyal.
Grooming: 🐾🐾
Feeding: 🐾🐾🐾
Exercise: 🐾🐾

Notes: Often dislikes being left alone for more than a short period. Can be clumsy and stubborn. Not the easiest breed to train.

◼ BULL TERRIER

Height: 46–61 cm
Weight: 24–28 kg
Average lifespan: 11–13 years
Temperament: Affectionate, intelligent, outgoing and lovable.
Grooming: 🐾
Feeding: 🐾🐾🐾
Exercise: 🐾🐾🐾🐾🐾

Notes: Great determination and stubbornness can make training difficult. Although not naturally quarrelsome, tends to react if challenged. Likely to become miserable and destructive if left to his own devices.

◼ CAVALIER KING CHARLES SPANIEL

Height: 24–34 cm
Weight: 5.5–8 kg
Average lifespan: 10–11 years
Temperament: Friendly, affectionate, fun-loving, biddable and charming.
Grooming: 🐾🐾
Feeding: 🐾🐾
Exercise: 🐾🐾

Notes: Full of life and easy to train. Loves human company of all ages; adaptable enough to fit in with either a family or a single older owner.

◼ CHIHUAHUA (Smooth-coated)

Height: 15–23 cm
Weight: 1–3 kg
Average lifespan: 13–15 years
Temperament: Alert, bold and spirited.
Grooming: 🐾
Feeding: 🐾
Exercise: 🐾

Notes: Not a good family dog, preferring a close one-to-one relationship. Barks readily and may be nervous and snappy with strangers and other dogs.

■ COCKER SPANIEL (English)

Height: 38–41 cm
Weight: 13–14.5 kg
Average lifespan: 9–15 years
Temperament: Gentle, affectionate, loyal and enthusiastic, with a happy nature and constantly wagging tail.
Grooming:
Feeding:
Exercise:
Notes: An energetic breed which dislikes being left alone. Keen to please, but has a sensitive nature which is easily upset by harsh treatment when training.

■ DACHSHUND (Standard Smooth-haired)

Height: 20–28 cm
Weight: 9–12 kg
Average lifespan: 14–16 years
Temperament: Faithful, versatile and good tempered.
Grooming:
Feeding:
Exercise:
Notes: Intelligent and courageous, can be vocal and still possesses a strong hunting instinct. Strong bonds may be formed with owner, but can be reserved with strangers.

■ DALMATIAN

Height: 56–61 cm
Weight: 23–25 kg
Average lifespan: 11–13 years
Temperament: Outgoing, friendly and highly affectionate.
Grooming:
Feeding:
Exercise:
Notes: Playful and boisterous, loves human company and dislikes being left alone. Easily bored and with tremendous stamina, this breed needs good training and plenty of exercise.

■ DOBERMANN PINSCHER

Height: 65–69 cm
Weight: 30–40 kg
Average lifespan: 10–12 years
Temperament: Intelligent, loyal and affectionate.
Grooming:
Feeding:
Exercise:
Notes: Bold, alert and strong-willed, quick to learn and highly trainable. Requires plenty of mental stimulation as well as physical exercise, positive training and calm, confident handling.

■ ENGLISH SETTER

Height: 61–69 cm
Weight: 25–30 kg
Average lifespan: 10–12 years
Temperament: Intensely friendly and good natured.
Grooming:
Feeding:
Exercise:
Notes: Very active and best suited to a country rather than a town lifestyle. Loves children and is relatively easy to train. Dislikes being left alone for extended periods and is liable to become excessively boisterous if lacking in exercise and attention.

■ ENGLISH SPRINGER SPANIEL

Height: 48–51 cm
Weight: 18–25 kg
Average lifespan: 13–14 years
Temperament: Lively, happy, friendly and sociable.
Grooming:
Feeding:
Exercise:
Notes: Always on the go and definitely not a breed for fair weather walkers or couch potatoes. Failure to provide sufficient physical and mental exercise can lead to destructive behaviour.

■ GERMAN SHEPHERD

Height: 58–63 cm
Weight: 34–43 kg
Average lifespan: 12–13 years
Temperament: Courageous, highly intelligent and loyal.
Grooming:
Feeding:
Exercise:
Notes: The Alsatian loves new challenges: essential to provide mental stimulation as well as physical exercise. Confident, consistent and positive leadership as well as commitment are required.

■ GOLDEN RETRIEVER

Height: 51–61 cm
Weight: 25–34 kg
Average lifespan: 12–13 years
Temperament: Gentle, friendly, intelligent and confident.
Grooming:
Feeding:
Exercise:
Notes: Versatility and trainability help make this an ideal as well as a popular family pet, but can be very exuberant as a puppy.

GREAT DANE

Height: 71–86 cm
Weight: 46–54 kg
Average lifespan: 7–10 years
Temperament: Alert, powerful and dignified.
Grooming: 🐾
Feeding: 🐾 🐾 🐾 🐾 🐾
Exercise: 🐾 🐾 🐾
Notes: Gentle giant with a calm and affectionate nature. Generally comfortable with children, strangers and other animals, but care needs to be taken as may accidentally cause injury due to large size.

GREYHOUND

Height: 69–76 cm
Weight: 27–32 kg
Average lifespan: 12–14 years
Temperament: Intelligent, gentle and affectionate.
Grooming: 🐾
Feeding: 🐾 🐾 🐾
Exercise: 🐾 🐾 🐾
Notes: Patient and gentle, needing less exercise than you might expect, although a suitable and safe space will be needed for off-leash running. Care must also be taken around small animals.

HUNGARIAN VISZLA

Height: 53–64 cm
Weight: 20–30 kg
Average lifespan: 10–14 years
Temperament: Lively, intelligent and affectionate.
Grooming: 🐾
Feeding: 🐾 🐾 🐾
Exercise: 🐾 🐾 🐾 🐾 🐾
Notes: Loves being outdoors and will require a good-sized garden and plenty of open space to meet exercise requirements. Sensitive and easy to train, but can be protective and vocal.

JACK RUSSELL

Height: 25–31 cm
Weight: 5.5–6.5 kg
Average lifespan: 14–15 years
Temperament: Cheeky, confident and alert.
Grooming: 🐾
Feeding: 🐾
Exercise: 🐾 🐾 🐾
Notes: Bold and active, but can be wilful and bossy, will not tolerate mishandling and can be short-tempered. Loves to dig, can be aggressive with other dogs and has a strong hunting instinct.

LABRADOR RETRIEVER

Height: 55–57 cm
Weight: 25–34 kg
Average lifespan: 10–12 years
Temperament: Good tempered, intelligent and eager to please.
Grooming: 🐾 🐾
Feeding: 🐾 🐾 🐾 🐾
Exercise: 🐾 🐾 🐾 🐾
Notes: A good family pet. Active, and often an enthusiastic swimmer. Easy to train, but tends to be greedy and can become overweight as an adult unless care is taken.

LHASA APSO

Height: 20–25 cm
Weight: 6–7 kg
Average lifespan: 13–14 years
Temperament: Friendly, outgoing and alert.
Grooming: 🐾 🐾 🐾 🐾 🐾
Feeding: 🐾 🐾
Exercise: 🐾
Notes: May be aloof with strangers, but loves being part of the family. Sometimes assertive and stubborn, and will become miserable if denied constant contact.

MALTESE

Height: 20–25 cm
Weight: 2–3 kg
Average lifespan: 11–14 years
Temperament: Lively, alert and charming.
Grooming: 🐾 🐾 🐾 🐾
Feeding: 🐾
Exercise: 🐾
Notes: Sweet tempered and intelligent, a gentle and sensitive companion who loves to please. Can be vocal and dislikes being left alone. Coat is high-maintenance if left long.

MINIATURE SCHNAUZER

Height: 33–36 cm
Weight: 6–7 kg
Average lifespan: 13–14 years
Temperament: Active, versatile, intelligent and loyal.
Grooming: 🐾 🐾 🐾
Feeding: 🐾 🐾
Exercise: 🐾 🐾 🐾
Notes: A lively breed needing plenty of mental stimulation as well as regular walks. Dislikes being left alone for long, and can sometimes be vocal.

NEWFOUNDLAND

Height: 66–71 cm
Weight: 50–68 kg
Average lifespan: 8–10 years
Temperament: Gentle, docile and happy nature.
Grooming: 🐾🐾🐾🐾🐾
Feeding: 🐾🐾🐾🐾🐾
Exercise: 🐾🐾🐾

Notes: Devoted family dog, but not for the housepround: produces lots of slobber and loves water, whether in a bowl, muddy puddle or river. Dislikes being left alone – great physical strength and large size belie a sensitive nature.

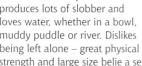

PEKINGESE

Height: 15–23 cm
Weight: 2.75–5.5 kg
Average lifespan: 10–14 years
Temperament: Fearless, aloof, loyal and intelligent.
Grooming: 🐾🐾🐾🐾🐾🐾
Feeding: 🐾
Exercise: 🐾

Notes: Regal, dignified, self-confident – but also possessing a sense of fun, and often devoted to his owner. Will not appreciate rough handling and requires patience when training.

POMERANIAN

Height: 18–28 cm
Weight: 1.5–3 kg
Average lifespan: 11–15 years
Temperament: Extrovert, intelligent and affectionate.
Grooming: 🐾🐾🐾🐾
Feeding: 🐾
Exercise: 🐾

Notes: Lively and loyal, a busy little dog who loves to be petted but can be vocal, wilful and is inclined to be bossy. Training is as important as with larger breeds if he is to be well-mannered.

POODLE (Standard)

Height: 38–66 cm
Weight: 20–32 kg
Average lifespan: 11–13 years
Temperament: Fun-loving and good natured.
Grooming: 🐾🐾🐾🐾🐾
Feeding: 🐾🐾🐾
Exercise: 🐾🐾🐾🐾

Notes: A highly trainable dog who enjoys plenty of attention and is eager to learn. The non-moulting coat will need regular clipping as well as daily grooming.

PUG

Height: 25–28 cm
Weight: 6.5–8 kg
Average lifespan: 12–13 years
Temperament: Friendly, tolerant, sociable and adaptable.
Grooming: 🐾🐾🐾
Feeding: 🐾
Exercise: 🐾🐾

Notes: Livelier than you might expect, a busy and enthusiastic pet who loves being part of the family and hates being excluded. A lot of energy is used up in play, so not overdemanding of exercise. Has a tendency to become overweight unless diet and exercise carefully regulated.

ROTTWEILER

Height: 58–69 cm
Weight: 41–54 kg
Average lifespan: 10–12 years
Temperament: Self-confident, brave, intelligent and loyal.
Grooming: 🐾
Feeding: 🐾🐾🐾🐾🐾
Exercise: 🐾🐾🐾🐾🐾

Notes: Leadership and calm, confident handling are essential. Although affection and cuddles are enjoyed, this is not a breed for novices or couch potatoes. Choose an established breeder whose puppies are renowned for sound temperaments.

SCOTTISH TERRIER

Height: 25–28 cm
Weight: 8.5–10.5 kg
Average lifespan: 12–14 years
Temperament: Loyal, faithful and courageous.
Grooming: 🐾🐾🐾
Feeding: 🐾🐾
Exercise: 🐾🐾

Notes: Bold, intelligent, tough and independent, able to fit happily into most lifestyles and always ready to go anywhere, any time. Protective, possessing hunting instincts and not the easiest to train, they may be aggressive with other dogs unless well socialized in early life.

SHETLAND SHEEPDOG

Height: 36–37 cm
Weight: 6.5–7 kg
Average lifespan: 11–14 years
Temperament: Alert, intelligent and affectionate.
Grooming: 🐾🐾🐾🐾🐾
Feeding: 🐾🐾
Exercise: 🐾🐾🐾

Notes: Sensitive by nature, willing to please, and loyal and affectionate towards owner, but may be reserved with strangers. Can be vocal, greedy and has a strong chasing instinct.

■ SHIH TZU

Height: 25–27 cm
Weight: 4.5–8 kg
Average lifespan: 12–15 years
Temperament: Affectionate, playful and good tempered.
Grooming: 🐾 🐾 🐾 🐾 🐾
Feeding: 🐾 🐾
Exercise: 🐾 🐾
Notes: Adores human company and hates being left alone for any length of time. Generally keen to please, but sometimes wilful. High-maintenance coat needs daily attention if left long, so many owners opt to clip it.

■ SIBERIAN HUSKY

Height: 51–60 cm
Weight: 16–27 kg
Average lifespan: 12–15 years
Temperament: Friendly, alert, affectionate and intelligent.
Grooming: 🐾 🐾
Feeding: 🐾 🐾 🐾 🐾
Exercise: 🐾 🐾 🐾 🐾 🐾
Notes: Poor recall (see page 91), so unreliable off-leash. An outstanding escape artist and keen hunter who is liable to become destructive, vocal and to self-mutilate if lonely. Needs a great deal of exercise. Not a breed for inactive or inexperienced owners.

■ STAFFORDSHIRE BULL TERRIER

Height: 35–41 cm
Weight: 11–17 kg
Average lifespan: 11–12 years
Temperament: Devoted, fun-loving, companionable and highly intelligent.
Grooming: 🐾
Feeding: 🐾 🐾 🐾 🐾
Exercise: 🐾 🐾 🐾 🐾
Notes: Active and muscular, needing to be well exercised both mentally and physically. Although generally loves people, care should be taken when meeting other dogs. Can be protective of the family.

■ WEIMARANER

Height: 56–69 cm
Weight: 32–39 kg
Average lifespan: 11–13 years
Temperament: Fearless, friendly and alert.
Grooming: 🐾
Feeding: 🐾 🐾 🐾 🐾
Exercise: 🐾 🐾 🐾 🐾 🐾
Notes: Intelligent, versatile and boisterous. Can be strong-willed, protective and may have a strong chasing instinct, so good training plus sufficient exercise essential.

■ WELSH CORGI (Pembroke)

Height: 25–31 cm
Weight: 9–12 kg
Average lifespan: 12–15 years
Temperament: Faithful, alert and intelligent.
Grooming: 🐾 🐾
Feeding: 🐾 🐾 🐾
Exercise: 🐾 🐾 🐾
Notes: Active, outgoing and reasonably easy to train, but care needed to ensure his bossiness doesn't get the upper hand. May also nip or herd when playing.

■ WEST HIGHLAND WHITE TERRIER

Height: 23–28 cm
Weight: 6–10 kg
Average lifespan: 12–14 years
Temperament: Tough, busy, curious and friendly.
Grooming: 🐾 🐾 🐾 🐾
Feeding: 🐾 🐾 🐾
Exercise: 🐾 🐾
Notes: Versatile, fun-loving family pet who loves to be involved in everything and will become unhappy if left alone for long periods. Can be single-minded and stubborn on occasion.

■ WHIPPET

Height: 44–51 cm
Weight: 12.5–13.5 kg
Average lifespan: 12–15 years
Temperament: Sensitive, gentle and affectionate.
Grooming: 🐾
Feeding: 🐾 🐾
Exercise: 🐾 🐾 🐾
Notes: Graceful, elegant and eager to please, enjoys company and is affectionate with familiar faces, although may be shy with strangers. Very strong chasing instinct, loves playing games and needs space in which to run.

■ YORKSHIRE TERRIER

Height: 18–25 cm
Weight: 1–3.25 kg
Average lifespan: 12–17 years
Temperament: Spirited, lively, devoted, alert.
Grooming: 🐾 🐾 🐾 🐾 🐾
Feeding: 🐾
Exercise: 🐾 🐾
Notes: Clever and affectionate, but can also be vocal, feisty and wilful. Although not overdemanding of exercise, nevertheless needs a busy, active lifestyle to prevent boredom and frustration.

Potential health problems

	Elbow Dysplasia	Hip Dysplasia	Eye Problems	Heart Problems	Blood Disorders	Skin Problems	Neurological Problems	Other
Airedale Terrier			●	●	●	●		
Basset Hound	●	●	●		●		●	Patellar luxation
Beagle			●	●	●		●	Hypothyroidism
Bernese Mountain Dog	●	●			●		●	Osteochondritis dissecans (OCD); bloat
Bichon Frise			●	●	●	●		
Border Collie			●		●		●	
Border Terrier			●		●			Kidney problems
Boston Terrier			●					Respiratory problems; various cancers; patellar luxation
Boxer				●	●			Respiratory problems; various cancers; hypothyroidism; bloat
Bulldog	●	●	●				●	Respiratory problems; various cancers
Bull Terrier			●		●	●	●	Stomach cancer; kidney problems
Cavalier King Charles Spaniel			●	●			●	Diabetes
Chihuahua			●	●	●		●	Narcolepsy; patellar luxation
Cocker Spaniel (English)			●	●	●	●	●	Kidney problems
Dachshund			●	●	●		●	Kidney problems; spinal problems
Dalmatian			●	●			●	Copper toxicosis; kidney problems; bloat
Dobermann			●	●	●		●	Hypothyroidism; narcolepsy; Wobbler syndrome; bloat
English Setter	●	●					●	Osteochondritis dissecans (OCD); hypothyroidism
English Springer Spaniel	●	●	●	●	●	●	●	Fucosidosis
German Shepherd	●	●	●	●	●		●	Panosteitis; bloat
Golden Retriever	●	●	●	●	●	●	●	Various cancers; osteochondritis dissecans (OCD)
Great Dane	●			●				Wobbler syndrome; bone cancer; bloat
Greyhound					●	●	●	Bone cancer
Hungarian Viszla				●		●	●	
Jack Russell			●					Patellar luxation
Labrador Retriever	●	●	●	●	●	●	●	Kidney problems; bloat
Lhasa Apso			●		●			Kidney problems; patellar luxation
Maltese				●	●		●	
Miniature Schnauzer			●	●	●		●	Diabetes; hypothyroidism
Newfoundland	●	●						Bone cancer; bloat
Pekingese			●					Respiratory problems; spinal problems; patellar luxation
Pomeranian			●	●	●		●	
Poodle (Standard)		●	●	●	●	●	●	Hypothyroidism; bloat
Pug		●	●		●		●	Cushing's disease; spinal problems; respiratory problems; diabetes; Legg-Calve Perthes disease
Rottweiler	●	●	●	●	●			Cancers; kidney problems; osteochondritis dissecans (OCD); bloat
Scottish Terrier					●		●	
Shetland Sheepdog		●	●	●	●		●	
Shih Tzu			●		●			Kidney problems
Siberian Husky			●		●		●	Diabetes
Staffordshire Bull Terrier			●				●	Stomach cancer
Weimaraner				●	●			Bloat; spinal problems
Welsh Corgi (Pembroke)					●		●	Various cancers
West Highland White Terrier			●		●		●	Copper toxicosis; kidney problems
Whippet			●	●				Cryptorchidism
Yorkshire Terrier			●	●	●			Legg-Calve Perthes disease; kidney problems; patellar luxation

This is not an exhaustive list of all the health issues to which the breed you are interested in may be susceptible, so you should do further research. Potential health problems for which screening schemes are available include hip and elbow dysplasia, and a range of eye disorders. Some DNA tests for certain hereditary diseases are also available to identify normal, carrier and affected dogs. Contact the appropriate breed club or view the Kennel Club website for further information on tests.

HOW TO FIND YOUR DOG

Taking on a dog is not only a big financial commitment, but also a major emotional one and you can quickly begin to bond with your new pet. Getting a dog from a reputable source is therefore important, as buying one who subsequently becomes ill will result in a lot of heartbreak as well as large veterinary bills.

Breeders

If you wish to purchase a pedigree puppy, you will need to find a breeder who is either planning a litter or has one ready for viewing. Some breeders are better than others; talk to as many people as possible who are knowledgeable about your chosen breed to find out which breeders have good reputations. Visit several so that you can compare litters, the conditions they are kept in, and to have a chat with the breeder about what you are looking for.

A good breeder will:

- Discuss breed requirements, problems and any potential health issues, and be prepared to show you any related screening certification.
- Want to know that a suitable home is being offered, so will ask you lots of searching questions.
- Not put you under pressure to take a puppy.
- Offer back-up if you have any difficulties, and be willing to take the puppy back if for some reason you find yourself unable to keep him.
- Ensure clean and tidy living conditions for the pups and their mother.
- Have nothing to hide – be wary if there is any reluctance to answer any of your questions.

Choose your puppy from a reputable breeder.

Breed rescues

If you would like to offer a home to a rescue dog, but have your heart set on a specific breed and can't find one at your local animal shelter, contact the relevant breed club. Virtually every breed has its own rescue organization, although availability is usually in proportion to the popularity of the breed; and while puppies are sometimes available, the majority are aged eight months and upwards. While a dog from a breed rescue organization will cost much less than from a breeder, a donation (on average around £100) is expected to help meet the expense of caring for the dog.

Waiting lists for prospective owners don't necessarily operate on a 'first come, first served' basis, but on the best match of dog and owner. Conditions are generally attached to adoption, such as undertaking to neuter and microchip the dog, and to return him to the rescue organization should you be unable to care for him at any future time. One of the advantages of breed rescue as opposed to an animal shelter is that the dog's background and the reason for his being handed in are often known.

Where to look

Contact details of breeders and animal shelters can be found in Yellow Pages, on the internet and in specialist dog magazines, as well as in local and national newspapers. Your local veterinary practice, local training clubs, other owners, pet shops, dog wardens and breed clubs may also be good sources of useful information.

Puppy farms

Puppies from puppy farms are to be avoided, as they will have been bred for the sole purpose of making money for the breeder and with little care for their health and well-being. Often kept in terrible conditions, separated too young from their mothers and transported long distances in cramped cages, they are likely to be sickly, full of worms, unvaccinated, liable to behaviour problems, and may also have inherited serious health issues from their parents. The only way to ensure you don't buy a puppy from such sources is to go to a reputable breeder.

Do not buy from the following sources, as they are likely to have acquired their puppies from a puppy farm:
- Pet shops: puppies are unlikely to have come from a breeder who cares what happens to them.
- Anyone advertising multiple breeds as opposed to one, or possibly two.
- Anyone who seems more interested in making a deal than in finding out if you can offer a suitable home.
- Anyone wanting to hand a pup over in a car park, or deliver it to your house. Never buy sight unseen – *always* make sure you see the pups with their mother.

Although some may be absolutely genuine, you should also be careful when responding to advertisements placed on the internet and in newspapers, as these are often ways in which pups from puppy farms are sold on. Be suspicious too of anyone who doesn't currently have a puppy for sale when contacted, but then suddenly finds one for you after all.

Rescue centres

Every year animal rescue centres are filled with thousands of unwanted dogs of all shapes, sizes and ages. Some are of mixed ancestry and others are pedigrees, but all have one thing in common: they desperately need a home. As with breed rescues, puppies are sometimes available but the majority are adolescent, adult or senior dogs.

A rescue dog will not be free, although he won't cost as much as a pedigree from a breeder. If your application is successful, you will be expected to make a donation (usually around £100) which helps to offset the cost of caring for the dog; it also ensures that you are making a serious commitment.

As with breeders, some rescue centres are better than others, so be prepared to visit several. A good centre will not only be clean, tidy and welcoming, but will also be able to advise and assist you in making the best choice.

HOW TO RECOGNIZE A GOOD CENTRE

- Staff will spend time chatting with you about the sort of dog you want, and you'll usually be asked to fill in a detailed questionnaire.
- Each dog will have been assessed to try to find out what sort of home would suit him best, and how he behaves with people, around food, toys, and with other dogs and animals.
- Staff will be happy to answer all your questions and to fill you in on the history of the dog as far as it is known.
- Dogs will have been given a health check by a vet, vaccinated, wormed and given any other treatment needed.
- An interim insurance scheme will be provided so that, until you've arranged a longer-term policy, your new dog will be covered during the first few weeks he is in your care.
- You will be required to sign documentation agreeing to certain conditions, such as neutering and microchipping the dog if this has not already been done, and to return the dog to the centre if for any reason you find yourself unable to keep him.
- Advice and guidance will be available if you have any problems.

WHAT WILL A GOOD CENTRE REQUIRE?

In order to protect their dogs, rescue centres usually have stringent criteria which they expect anyone wishing to adopt a pet from them to meet. Most centres won't rehome a dog to anyone under the age of 18, on income support, or if the dog will be left on his own for more than four hours each day. Some may also refuse to let you adopt a dog if you have young children.

In addition, the centre will also want to see some form of ID and, if you don't own your house, written confirmation from your landlord that you are permitted to keep a dog. Finally, before being allowed to take a dog away, a date will be made for someone appointed by the centre to visit your home to check that it is indeed suitable.

Rescue dogs can be loyal and loving companions.

VISITING A BREEDER

Having found a reputable breeder whom you like and feel you can trust – and provided you also meet his or her exacting standards as a potential owner – then your next big decision is to pick out a puppy.

Viewing a litter

When the breeder lets you know that the puppies are old enough for you to view, make an appointment to visit. If you have children, don't take them with you, as the need to keep an eye on them can be distracting and they may also sway you against your better judgement into making the wrong choice.

When you arrive, you should be able to see the puppies with their mother. Introduce yourself to her first before turning your attention to the youngsters.

Give her time to get used to your presence, as she may be a little protective of the pups at first. She should appear in good health, confident and friendly – her demeanour can be an indicator of the temperament and behaviour her offspring are likely to inherit.

Observing the puppies

The easiest way to start finding out more about the puppies is by getting down to their level – you're less likely accidentally to step on one and you'll get a better view when sitting down. If you want to pick one up to examine him more closely, always ask the breeder first. Puppies can wriggle and squirm a lot when picked up, and dropping one could seriously injure or even kill him, so place him on your lap while you sit on the floor, rather than holding him while you stand.

Make sure you are able to view the mother with the puppies.

Questions to ask

In all the excitement of choosing a puppy, it can be easy to forget to ask for more information about the litter. Jot a few questions down on a piece of paper in advance of your visit so that you have something to jog your memory, including:

- Have any health checks appropriate to the breed been carried out, and can you see the relevant certification?
- What worming and/or vaccinations have the puppies received?
- What socialization has the breeder done with the puppies? A good breeder will have tried to expose them to a variety of new experiences so that the sights, sounds and smells in your home won't be alarming. If the puppies have been kept kennelled outdoors they should have been brought into the house for periods each day.
- Will there be any temporary insurance cover for the first few weeks until you can sort out your own? Most good breeders usually subscribe to some sort of scheme.
- Will there be any support and advice should you need it, and will the breeder be willing to take the dog back should you find yourself unable to keep him for any reason?
- What type of written guarantee and contract will be provided?

Get down to puppy level to introduce yourself.

Choosing a puppy

Spend some time with all the puppies before choosing the one you want. Talk to the breeder about them as well, asking advice on which one might be best suited to you, as he or she will be familiar with their individual characters.

LOOK FOR PERSONALITY TRAITS

The puppies will tend to be energetic in spurts, rather than constantly on the go – but while they are active, observe how they interact with each other. At this age they all look irresistibly cute, but they'll also be exhibiting definite personality traits which can help you choose between them.

The puppies should be alert, curious and responsive to noises around them; note any who seem timid, indifferent, bossy or pushy, as these qualities may become more pronounced as the puppy gets older. If you are new to owning a dog, then ideally you want to select the 'easy' one who will be least likely to present you with behavioural or training difficulties and will grow up to become a well-rounded individual.

HOW DOES THE PUPPY RESPOND?

As well as watching how the puppies behave with each other, notice how they respond to your presence. They should be happy to be around you, with no objection to being picked up and handled. Hold each in turn on your lap, gently take each paw and look in their ears; they should be relaxed and trusting, not trying to chew you ferociously to bits or panicking. Drop a bunch of keys on the floor to see how they react to noise as well; they may understandably be startled, but shouldn't be terrified.

IS THE PUPPY HEALTHY?

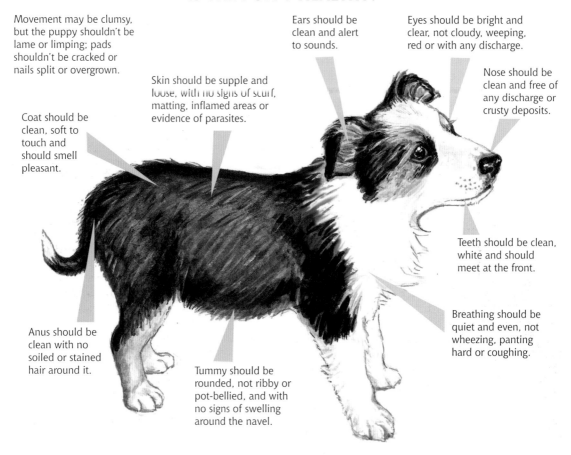

Movement may be clumsy, but the puppy shouldn't be lame or limping; pads shouldn't be cracked or nails split or overgrown.

Skin should be supple and loose, with no signs of scurf, matting, inflamed areas or evidence of parasites.

Coat should be clean, soft to touch and should smell pleasant.

Ears should be clean and alert to sounds.

Eyes should be bright and clear, not cloudy, weeping, red or with any discharge.

Nose should be clean and free of any discharge or crusty deposits.

Teeth should be clean, white and should meet at the front.

Breathing should be quiet and even, not wheezing, panting hard or coughing.

Anus should be clean with no soiled or stained hair around it.

Tummy should be rounded, not ribby or pot-bellied, and with no signs of swelling around the navel.

AFTER YOU'VE CHOSEN

Once you've made your choice, you'll need to leave a deposit, with the balance payable when you return to collect the puppy. Ask if it will be possible to visit again once or twice so you are able to get to know the puppy a little better and can introduce other family members to him. Leave a towel or old blanket with the puppy which you can collect at the same time as you pick him up; it will by then smell of him and his siblings, and the familiar scent will be comforting when he goes to his new home.

Choosing a rescue dog

Many dogs find themselves in rescue centres through no fault of their own. An owner's loss of income, illness or death, or a move to accommodation where pets aren't welcome are all common causes. Other rescue dogs may be unclaimed strays with no known background, or handed in because the owner was unable to cope with the unanticipated challenges of an energetic and demanding adolescent. In the right homes they can make loving and very rewarding pets, although sometimes remedial training may be required.

VISITING A RESCUE CENTRE

When visiting a rescue centre you will need to choose wisely and carefully. Although you need to feel attracted to the dog you choose, you shouldn't pick one just because you feel sorry for him. Because it's not always easy to be guided by your head as much as your heart in such situations, prepare yourself before you go by drawing up a list of all the things you do and don't want. This will make it easier for kennel staff to direct you towards those dogs most likely to fit the bill.

Allow plenty of time for your visit – this is an important decision and not one to hurry. Weekends and holidays are usually very busy, so if possible call in on a weekday, having first checked on opening hours.

Procedure varies between centres, but on arrival you will usually be asked to fill in a fairly detailed questionnaire, which may be followed by a personal interview. A good centre will be as particular as any breeder about the homes their dogs go to. At some centres you can walk round to view all the dogs available for adoption, but at others those dogs that are thought to be the best match will be brought out to meet you instead.

Try to avoid acting on impulse. Spend as much time as possible getting to know any dog you are interested in to be sure you click with each other.

Behaviour problems

When you take home a rescue dog, there's a good chance that you'll be taking home emotional and behaviour problems too. Although staff at the centre should have done their best to assess each animal in their care, some dogs may begin to behave differently once settled into their new home. Sometimes this change can be for the better, but it can also mean the appearance of an undesirable behaviour. The good news is that most behaviour problems can be remedied with patience, consistency and common sense, and a good rescue centre will be able to offer you advice and support if needed. But don't take on a dog with known behaviour problems unless you feel experienced and committed enough to cope, and do discuss the matter first with staff who are familiar with the dog. For more on problem behaviours, see Chapter 6.

FINDING OUT MORE

Find out as much as you can about the dogs you are interested in. Ask about any known background, what assessment has been done, and how long the dog has been at the centre. If you have any specific requirements, such as a dog that is good with children or other pets, make sure you emphasize and double-check these points.

Take as much time as you can getting to know each of the dogs you have shortlisted. Some may be very stressed by living in kennels. Ask if there is somewhere you can go where it is a bit quieter so you can find out about each other away from all the bustle and activity. There may be a room or enclosed paddock area set aside for this, as well as somewhere you can go for a walk together.

Introduce yourself quietly, and then try a little interaction, petting, playing and walking with the dog to find out if you click with each other. The dog should be interested in you and enjoy all the attention and handling. If he seems scared, is at all aggressive or just isn't interested in being with you, then keep on looking.

DECISION TIME

It may make you feel mean, but don't feel obliged to take whatever dog you're offered if you don't feel he's 'the one'. Take comfort from the thought that, although he may not be right for you, someone else will think he's perfect and will give him a great home. Continue your own search until you do find a dog you really gel with.

Having made your choice, you will need to introduce the rest of your family, and any other pets you own, to ensure that they are as happy with the prospective new arrival as you are.

Chapter 2

ALL ABOUT YOUR DOG

A dog is not a wolf any more than a wolf is a dog. In order to make them safer to live with and better at helping us with a wide variety of tasks, dogs have been changed considerably from their wild relatives. Selective breeding practices have exaggerated characteristics we want and diminished those considered undesirable. Yet despite many differences, the shared common heritage can't be completely ignored and plenty of behavioural similarities are still evident. These need to be recognized and outlets provided for them, as lack of opportunity to indulge in instinctive behaviours can lead to frustration and the development of 'problem' behaviours.

Knowing a little about how your dog evolved into the animal he is today and how his body works will help you understand how he perceives the world around him and why he acts in ways that can sometimes seem baffling to us. This in turn will help you care for him better and train him successfully, and will allow both of you to enjoy each other's company to the full.

WHERE YOUR DOG COMES FROM

One of the first species to be domesticated, dogs have forged deep bonds with us during the many thousands of years of our relationship. Rising from the position of mere scavenger, the dog has gone on to become an invaluable co-worker and helpmate, as well as finding a place in our hearts as a close companion.

15,000 years ago

First archaeological evidence of domestication, although genetic evidence suggests that dogs diverged from wolves far earlier than this – possibly as long as 135,000 years ago in East Asia. Nobody knows exactly how our relationship starts, although it's generally speculated that wolves are attracted by easy opportunities for scavenging and begin living in close proximity to groups of humans. Their presence is tolerated as it helps keep vermin down; they also prove useful in warning of the approach of intruders, both two- and four-footed. Those least fearful of humans and non-threatening in behaviour profit most and gradually become increasingly tame.

4,500 BC

The first 'dogs' still look like wolves, but as humans change from a hunter-gatherer lifestyle to a more settled agricultural existence, so dogs begin to change shape. As Man starts to realize their potential and to breed selectively for specific tasks, five distinct types of dog come into being: mastiffs, wolf-type dogs, sighthounds, pointers and herding dogs.

18th century

Although breeding for and exaggerating certain physical and behavioural characteristics produce definite types of dog that are highly successful at carrying out specialized tasks, recognizable breeds within these groups begin to emerge only during the 1700s.

1859

The first organized dog show is held in the UK, at Newcastle upon Tyne. Only 60 entries are exhibited, all of them Pointers and Setters.

1873

As showing becomes an increasingly popular pastime, the Kennel Club is formed in the UK, followed in 1884 by the foundation of the American Kennel Club. Emphasis is placed on developing and maintaining recognizable 'pure-bred' animals, and standards are drawn up setting out the requirements for each breed.

Present day

Unfortunately, not all changes that have been made to produce pedigree breeds have been in the best interests of the dogs: many health problems have arisen due to breeding for specific looks. Happily, current trends are towards encouraging the breeding of healthier animals with less exaggerated features.

Jobs for dogs

The dog's earliest job may have been as camp scavenger, but since then his versatility and adaptability have enabled him to fulfil a number of varied roles, including hunting, guarding, pulling loads, herding and protection. In wartime he has served as fighter, messenger and sentry, while in peacetime he has been used to apprehend criminals; to search out weapons, drugs and other contraband; for rescue work; and he has even been sent into space.

Dogs have also proved their worth as Guide, Hearing, Assistance and Therapy dogs. More recently their superb powers of observation and smell have made it possible to train them to alert owners with epilepsy of imminent seizures and to detect cancer through sniffing urine samples.

The wolf inside

Many wolf characteristics have either diminished or disappeared entirely – some because they are no longer needed for survival, others as a direct result of artificial selection by mankind. Others still remain, although in a modified form.

PHYSICAL DIFFERENCES

The most striking differences between dogs and wolves are physical:

- **Wolves are seasonal breeders:** bitches come into season once a year in spring and produce between two and four cubs.
- **Dogs produce litters at any time of year:** bitches of most breeds generally come into season twice a year and have from three to eight or more pups.
- **Wolves have larger teeth and more powerful jaws:** their biting capacity is 1,000–1,500 lb pressure/square inch, which enables them to shear a deer leg in half with ease. A dog's smaller teeth and jaws reduce bite capacity to 750 lb/square inch for a German Shepherd. (In humans it is a mere 300 lb/square inch.)
- **Dogs have smaller skulls:** 20 per cent smaller than those of wolves.
- **Dogs have smaller brains:** 10 per cent smaller than those of wolves.
- **Wolf paws are larger:** nearly twice the size of those of similar-sized dogs.
- **Dogs have a wider variety of size, shape and coat colours:** wolves do vary in size and coat colour, but not so much as dogs.

BEHAVIOURAL SIMILARITIES

Although there are plenty of physical differences, dogs retain numerous wolf-like behavioural traits – although many, such as barking, are more akin to a juvenile than to an adult wolf. Others are partial behaviours; for example, the slinking posture adopted by a Border Collie as he circles a flock of sheep or isolates an individual has its roots in the way a wolf stalks its prey – but without the kill. Other innate wolf-like behaviours are:

- **Chasing moving objects:** another animal, a cyclist, a jogger or a ball.
- **Creating a food stash:** burying food in the garden or even beneath a cushion in the house.
- **Scent-marking territory with urine.**
- **Digging a shallow hole to lie in** during hot weather.
- **Circling** to make a comfortable nest before lying down to sleep.
- **Creating a den:** under a table or bed, or in a crate.
- **Rolling in smelly things.**
- **Scavenging food:** including stale food and carrion.

Belyaev's foxes

An experiment begun in 1959 by scientist Dmitri Belyaev helps show how quickly domestication can happen and the way it influences physical and behavioural characteristics. Belyaev bred silver foxes – a species that had never before been domesticated – with tameness the sole criterion for selecting individuals for breeding. Within 10 generations the silver foxes were exhibiting similar behavioural characteristics to domestic dogs: eager to meet people, affectionate towards their keepers, wagging their tails and whimpering to attract attention. Physical changes became apparent too – floppy ears, curled tails, spotted and black-and-white coats – and the domesticated foxes produced different levels of hormones from their wild counterparts.

Burying food is an inherited wolf behaviour.

LIFECYCLE

The normal length of pregnancy in dogs is 59–65 days, although this can vary. At birth the puppies are virtually helpless but, compared to humans, they then develop very quickly.

From birth to maturity

3 hours The puppy is blind, deaf and toothless, but has his sense of taste. He can sense being touched on his head. Along with scent and heat sensors in the nose, this sense allows him to detect his mother and crawl over to her. Close contact helps calm and relax them both, as well as making the youngster feel safe. He can raise his head and if he rolls over is able to turn himself the right way up again.

1 week Still largely helpless, he spends 90 per cent of his time sleeping and the rest suckling. Mother stimulates the pup to urinate and defecate by licking his genitals; she then consumes the waste. This instinctive behaviour, designed to conceal the presence of pups from predators, is continued until her offspring are 3–4 weeks old.

2 weeks Touch reflexes develop in the front legs and the pup can sit up. At 8–10 days the eyes open, although vision is limited. At 12–16 days the ear canals open and the puppy hears for the first time.

3 weeks Touch reflexes are now developed in the back legs and the puppy is able to stand. Coordination of movement quickly develops. The pup's brain and nerves now register pain as quickly as those of an adult dog. Milk teeth start to appear.

4 weeks Vision well developed at 4–5 weeks. The pup is more active, learning to play and interact with littermates. Mother spends more time away from the puppies.

6 weeks Reflexes, balance, coordination and confidence all continue to develop. The puppy begins to investigate his surroundings. Weaning can start.

7–8 weeks Nervous system has reached maturity and by 8 weeks the puppy is usually ready to go to his new home. At this age he is very adaptable.

8–18 weeks Period of rapid learning during which it is important to socialize the puppy if he is going to grow into a confident, well-adjusted adult. A brief 'fearful' stage when he is easily scared often occurs at around 10 weeks. More information on socialization can be found on pages 75–76.

4–6 months Adult teeth start to appear. The puppy begins testing the limits of permitted behaviour as he becomes more independent. At around 4 months he may go through a second 'fearful' stage when meeting strangers and in new situations.

6–9 months The adolescent phase; females may have their first season, while males will start showing masculine behaviour.

1 year old Rapid-growth phase ends and the puppy is now technically an adult, albeit a young one, not yet fully mature either physically or mentally.

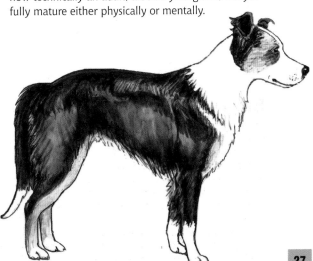

How long do dogs live?

The average lifespan of a dog is between 10 and 12 years, but this varies according to size and breed. Smaller dogs generally live longer than bigger ones, even though they reach maturity earlier. Insurance companies classify most dogs as 'seniors' or 'veterans' at the age of seven or eight – or at five or six years old in the case of the shorter-lived giant breeds.

The effects of ageing are similar to those experienced by humans, including arthritis, deterioration of vision and hearing, incontinence and senility. See Chapter 8 for more on elderly dogs.

Elderly dogs need extra care.

Dog years and their human equivalent

By the time they are a year old, most breeds have reached their full height and are sexually active, although they may still need to broaden out and put on muscle. Emotional maturity is generally reached at around 18 months–2 years. If you aren't sure how old your dog is, you can hazard a guess by looking to see how many milk teeth are present. After the first year estimates will be less accurate, based on wear and tear on the adult teeth and any tartar present, and also taking into account general bodily condition. The table below shows the rate at which dogs of different sizes age in comparison to humans.

The oldest dog

The Guinness World Record for the oldest dog is held by Bluey, an Australian Cattle Dog from Victoria. Born on 7 June 1910, he herded cattle for 20 years before retiring. He died on 14 November 1939, aged 29 years and 5 months.

	Human age equivalent			
Real years	Small (0–9 kg)	Medium (10–23 kg)	Large (24–40 kg)	Giant (over 40 kg)
1	15	14	14	12
2	24	21	20	19
3	28	26	26	26
4	32	31	32	33
5	36	36	38	40
6	40	41	44	47
7	44	46	50	54
8	48	51	56	61
9	52	56	62	68
10	56	61	68	75
11	60	66	74	82
12	64	71	80	89
13	68	76	86	96
14	72	81	92	103
15	76	86	98	110

SKELETON

Your dog's skeleton provides a framework that gives shape to his body, helps protect his internal organs, supports his weight and, together with the muscles, facilitates movement. His bones also act as a storehouse for calcium, phosphorus and many other elements.

Your dog's bones

A dog has around 320 bones; you have about 206. The number varies depending on whether he has extra toes (see page 31) and how long his tail is.

All about your dog

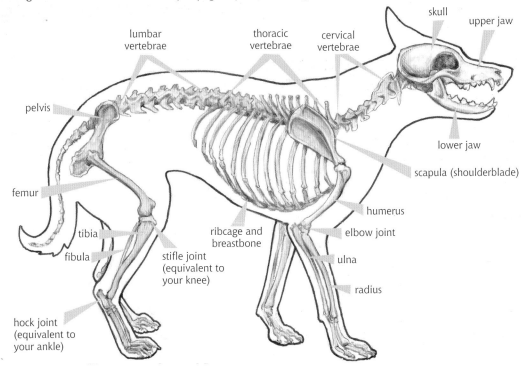

lumbar vertebrae — thoracic vertebrae — cervical vertebrae — skull — upper jaw — lower jaw — scapula (shoulderblade) — humerus — elbow joint — ulna — radius — ribcage and breastbone — stifle joint (equivalent to your knee) — fibula — tibia — femur — pelvis — hock joint (equivalent to your ankle)

Skeletal problems

It takes longer – up to 18 months – for the bones and joints of large and giant breeds to mature than those of smaller dogs. During this period of growth it's important to try to reduce the risk of bone deformities by minimizing stresses caused by excessive exercise or games involving jumping. Accelerated growth caused by diets too rich in calories or minerals has also been linked to skeletal problems, with bones that are less able to withstand stresses, so careful feeding is needed (see pages 61–64).

Missing bone

Dogs have no equivalent of our own collarbone. This increases length of stride and flexibility when turning, and allows maximum shock absorption when running, jumping, chasing and overcoming prey.

The tallest and the smallest

The smallest breed of dog is the Chihuahua, weighing only 1–3 kg. The tallest is the Irish Wolfhound, which stands 71–89 cm at the shoulder.

Skull shape

Skull shapes vary with breed and fall into three categories:

Dolichocephalic: long-nosed breeds, such as Sighthounds and Collies.

Brachycephalic: short-nosed breeds, such as Bulldogs and Pugs.

Mesocephalic: breeds that fall somewhere between these two extremes, such as Pointers.

As well as affecting appearance, skull shape also directly affects vision, scenting ability and heat regulation. Short-nosed breeds are more at risk of overheating during hot weather, have smaller olfactory areas (see page 36) than the other two types, less peripheral vision, and also often suffer from overcrowded teeth.

MUSCLES

Your dog has over 500 muscles, which make up half of his total body weight and enable him to walk, run and jump. They are also important for maintaining bodily functions such as the passage of food through the gut.

Your dog's muscles

Muscles in the tail make it capable of finely graded movements that help your dog communicate with others. The tail is also an important balancing aid while running and turning at speed, and acts as a rudder when swimming.

Skeletal muscle makes up the bulk of the musculature; these are muscles that can be contracted or relaxed at will.

Over a dozen muscles allow your dog to tilt, rotate and raise each ear independently, helping him to pinpoint the direction from which a sound is coming.

'**Invisible muscles**'. Like you, your dog also has 'involuntary' muscles – cardiac (heart muscles) and smooth (intestines, stomach and bladder).These help keep the internal organs functioning without him being conscious of it.

Forward movement for running and jumping is created chiefly by the powerful muscles of the hindquarters.

Front leg muscles are responsible for shock absorption and slowing down.

Fastest and highest

The fastest breed of dog is the Greyhound, which can reach speeds of up to 40 m.p.h. The world record for canine high jump is also held by a Greyhound, named Cindy, who cleared 172.7 cm in 2003.

Muscles and movement

Muscles involved in locomotion usually connect two bones and are generally arranged in pairs with an opposing effect: one flexes a limb while the other straightens it. Muscles are attached to bones by tendons; both these and ligaments (which attach bones to bones) are tough and fibrous. Unlike the muscles, they don't have a good blood supply, so if they sustain an injury they tend to heal slowly and need sufficient rest to allow this to happen.

Warming up before exercise reduces the risk of injury.

WARMING UP

As any human athlete knows, tissues that aren't properly prepared for exertion are more at risk of strain or serious injury. Your dog is no exception, so before any strenuous exercise – whether playing with a ball or Frisbee, or taking part in a competition – spend a little time giving him a warm-up. This raises the temperature in the muscles and increases blood circulation (and hence the availability of oxygen and other nutrients to the muscles) and ensures the joints are lubricated and supple. An effective warm-up is also associated with an increase in muscle strength and speed, so if you are competing with your dog in an activity such as agility, flyball or cani-cross, it can even improve performance.

Warm up by spending at least 10–15 minutes walking your dog on the leash, starting at a steady pace and gradually increasing it so he can move at a gentle jog before letting him run loose. After vigorous exercise, warming down (walking until his breathing has returned to normal) will help remove the waste products of exercise so that your dog is less likely to feel sore later.

PAWS AND CLAWS

Your dog doesn't just use his paws to get around; they also help him
in activities such as digging, swimming and even in scent-marking.

Your dog's paws

The **nail** on each toe grows continuously and, unless worn back by
contact with hard ground, will need regular trimming (see page 67).
If allowed to become too long, nails can force a dog to rock back on
his paws, causing strain and interfering with movement; long nails
are also more likely to snag on objects and get broken.

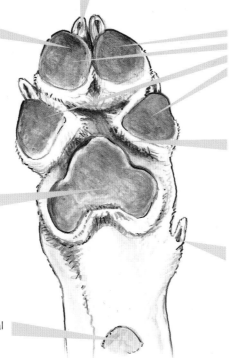

Digital pads on the underside
of the paws help with shock
absorption, as well as protecting
the inner structures and
providing traction. Although the
skin of the pads is tougher than
elsewhere on the body, it can
still be vulnerable to injury and
feet should be checked daily for
cuts and abrasions.

Metacarpal pads function like
the digital pads. They contain
sweat glands to keep them
supple and to leave odour
behind; some dogs scratch the
ground, kicking up soil with their
back paws, as well as urine-
marking, to notify other dogs of
their presence.

The **carpal pad** is used for additional
traction when stopping

Four toes on each paw make
contact with the ground. During
summer check for grass seeds, which
can sometimes work their way up
under the skin between each toe,
causing painful abscesses.

Hair between the toes and pads; in
winter this can collect mud, ice and
snow, which balls up into hard,
uncomfortable lumps. Trimming off
excess hair with scissors will prevent
this, but be patient and careful when
doing it as many dogs have very
ticklish feet.

An 'extra' toe, called the **dewclaw**,
is present on the front legs, and in
some breeds on the rear legs as well
(see below).

PAW SHAPE

Feet vary in shape according to breed; some are round
and cat-like in appearance, while others have longer
central toes with a shape described as 'harefoot'. Many
breeds that work in water have webbed feet, such as the
Newfoundland, Chesapeake Bay Retriever and
Portuguese Water Dog.

Left or right paw?

When it comes to
using their paws to
manoeuvre or
investigate something,
dogs appear to show a
definite preference,
with 80 per cent being
left-pawed.

DEWCLAWS

Dewclaws are vestigial toes present on the front legs, and
equivalent to our thumbs. Usually properly formed with
joints and tucked in close to the inner side of the leg
above the paw, they can be used to help grip bones and
other items that the dog is chewing.

Less commonly,
dewclaws can also
appear on the back legs –
several breeds are even
noted for having double
dewclaws, including the
Beauceron, Briard and
Pyrenean Mountain Dog.
Rear dewclaws are
positioned higher on the
leg and are often less
well developed than
those on the front.

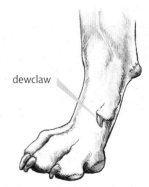

dewclaw

SKIN AND FUR

Skin is the largest organ of your dog's body. It forms a barrier between the outside world and the internal tissues and organs, has millions of nerve endings that tell him about his environment and is the site of vitamin D synthesis.

Your dog's skin structure

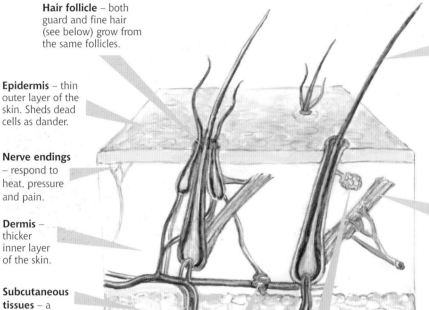

Hair follicle – both guard and fine hair (see below) grow from the same follicles.

Epidermis – thin outer layer of the skin. Sheds dead cells as dander.

Nerve endings – respond to heat, pressure and pain.

Dermis – thicker inner layer of the skin.

Subcutaneous tissues – a reservoir for fat, providing insulation and an energy store.

Hair – helps protect the skin from injury and UV radiation in sunlight, as well as retaining warmth; some coats manage this more efficiently than others. Most breeds moult in spring and autumn.

Arrector pili muscles – attach to hair follicles, when triggered by cold, fear or anger they contract and pull the hair upright.

Blood vessels – transport oxygen and nutrients to the skin cells and waste products away from them.

Sweat glands – present only in the skin forming the pads of the feet (see page 31).

Sebaceous glands – release an oily fluid with anti-microbial properties which helps keep the skin supple and waterproof. The secretions also function as **pheromones** – chemical substances detected by scent – which provide information and influence behaviour in other animals of the same species.

Hair types

Your dog has three different hair types:

Tactile hairs, also called **vibrissae**, are special extra-thick and long 'feeler' hairs found on the head which help your dog learn about his surroundings (see page 40).

Guard or primary hairs make up the top outer coat and are the type of hairs found on single-coated dogs, such as Whippets.

Fine or secondary hairs are soft, woolly hairs that make up the dense undercoat of double-coated breeds, such as German Shepherds.

All three hair types are clearly visible in this dog's coat.

Dogs with short, fine coats may need the extra warmth of a jacket during cold weather.

Dogs and allergy sufferers

The good news is that dogs are less likely to cause an allergic reaction than cats; the bad news is that there's no such thing as a completely hypoallergenic dog (one that won't cause an allergic reaction in a sufferer).

It's not actually the hair that causes the problems, but rather the dander (dead dried skin flakes). Allergens can also be found in the saliva and urine.

However, those breeds that shed minimally, have a short single coat or are hairless are less likely to cause problems.

Coat types

Type and length of hair contribute to the variety of different coat appearances. For example, Poodles have coats predominantly made up of particularly long, fine, curly hairs, while the Dobermann Pinscher is covered with short guard hairs.

Density of hair also affects the look and function of the coat: some northern breeds, such as the Siberian Husky, may have as many as 600 hairs per square centimetre of skin, while other breeds, such as the Yorkshire Terrier, may have as few as 100.

Dogs with no downy undercoat and only short single coats often feel the cold considerably during winter and will appreciate the warmth and protection provided by wearing a man-made jacket.

Heat loss

Dogs sweat only through glands in the pads of their feet, so they cool off in a different way from us. Primarily this is done by panting to increase the airflow over the moist surfaces of the tongue, throat and windpipe, so that heat is lost through evaporation (see page 35). Panting can also be an indicator of pain, fear or stress.

Dogs tolerate heat less well than we do, and those that are young, old, overweight or have short noses are especially at risk of heatstroke during hot weather.

Short-nosed dogs are particularly at risk of overheating if they do not have enough shade in hot weather.

THE BRAIN

The brain receives and registers sensory impulses such as sight, sound, taste, smell, touch and pain, decides what action to take and then causes the action to happen. It also controls automatic bodily functions and is the seat of learning and emotion.

Your dog's control centre

Your dog's brain is his control centre; it assesses all the information sent to it and sends out 'instructions' to the body. Different parts of the brain are in charge of dealing with different information.

Thalamus – relays sensory information to the **cortex** (the outer surface of the cerebrum); also responsible for enabling your dog to focus selectively and concentrate on one thing at a time.

Cerebrum – forms the bulk of the brain and is involved with learning, sensory perception, consciousness, decision-making and initiation of voluntary movements.

Cerebellum – mainly responsible for coordination of movement and posture.

Brain stem – controls various functions of the head, as well as heart rate and respiration. All nerves that connect to the facial muscles come from here.

Hypothalamus – collects information about the internal well-being of the body and uses it to control the release of hormones by the pituitary gland. Regulates appetite, thirst, body temperature, sleep cycles and reproduction.

Pituitary gland – produces hormones affecting growth, reproduction and stress responses.

Spinal cord – carries messages to the brain from the rest of the body and vice versa.

Brain function

Your dog's brain is small compared to yours. It weighs approximately 0.5 per cent of his body weight, whereas your brain is more than 2 per cent of your body weight. Despite its small size, it consumes around 20 per cent of the oxygen in the blood, and if deprived of oxygen for as little as 20 seconds, irreversible brain damage can occur.

How intelligent are dogs?

It is difficult to evaluate canine intelligence in comparison to ours, as dogs perceive the world differently from us and their priorities often differ too. However, studies have suggested that the average dog has an IQ equivalent to that of a three-year-old child.

Certain breeds have a reputation for being brighter than others, but success in any type of test set to try to determine intelligence depends on how strongly motivated the dog is to try it in the first place, as well as on natural aptitude. Ability can also vary considerably within, as well as between, breeds.

All dogs have an ability to learn, though, and even old dogs can be taught new tricks, although it may take a little longer for them to learn.

Can dogs suffer from mental health problems?

Like us, dogs can experience behavioural and emotional disorders, including phobias, stress and depression. Mental function can also deteriorate with age and some elderly dogs may suffer from senility (see page 123).

Problem-solving toys can be a good way of providing mental stimulation and preventing boredom.

TASTE AND THE MOUTH

Your dog has a more limited sense of taste than you do, tending to rely on his powerful sense of smell to tell him whether something is good to eat. He also uses his lips, tongue and teeth in the same way as we would our hands, to explore and find out more about new objects.

Your dog's sense of taste

The sense of taste is present in a dog right from birth, and is much better than that of a cat, although not as well developed as yours. His tongue has around 1,700 taste buds for processing flavours, compared to 473 in felines and 9,000 in humans.

Like you, your dog can detect sweet, sour, bitter and salty tastes. He will intensely dislike things that taste bitter and prefer meaty foodstuffs – although without using his nose as well he is unable to distinguish between different types. Many dogs also have something of a sweet tooth – a result of their heritage as scavengers as well as hunters, when fruit and berries would have formed part of their diet.

As a dog exercises, the flow of blood to his tongue can increase sixfold.

Tongue

The tongue is controlled by eight pairs of muscles and kept moist by four pairs of salivary glands. As well as responding to taste, it helps guide food into the mouth and assists in chewing and swallowing. It is also used to groom and clean parts of the body, to explore objects, and curls backwards to act as a ladle when drinking.

Very importantly, the tongue also plays a major part in heat loss. Heat causes the blood vessels to dilate, so the tongue swells and extends. Air passing over the tongue and the evaporation of saliva then allow the blood to be cooled, in the same way as sweating increases our own ability to lose heat.

Teeth

Your dog will have two sets of teeth during his lifetime. At around four months old the milk teeth begin to fall out and are replaced by larger adult teeth; the first to be shed are the incisors and the last to erupt are the molars. Most adult dogs have 42 teeth, which have different functions:

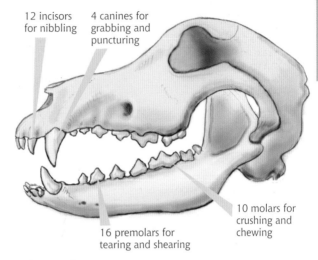

12 incisors for nibbling

4 canines for grabbing and puncturing

10 molars for crushing and chewing

16 premolars for tearing and shearing

Chewing

Chewing is a natural activity for puppies to indulge in when they are teething, as it helps relieve discomfort and aids in shedding the milk teeth. As chewing causes the release of chemicals called **endorphins**, which have a calming 'feel-good' effect, it is also a pleasurable activity for dogs of all ages and can be a coping mechanism resorted to when feeling bored, lonely, anxious or frustrated.

As well as providing your dog with an outlet for his innate desire to chew, giving him chewy treats and toys that have a flossing action will help to keep his teeth clean.

Provide suitable toys and treats to help your puppy exercise his teeth.

35

SMELL

Your dog has a very powerful sense of smell. Large noses are keener than small ones, but even the tiniest is far superior to ours. This has made dogs invaluable in helping us with tasks such as locating people, bombs, drugs and illicit foodstuffs.

How your dog smells

Cerebrum – one third of your dog's brain is set aside for scent detection alone.

Olfactory bulb – processes smells received from scent-detecting receptors in the nasal membranes, then passes the information to the brain for further analysis.

Frontal sinus – cavities in the bones around the nose help improve the sense of smell.

Nasal membranes – these cover the wafer-thin **turbinate bones** in the nose. If unfolded, they would cover an area the size of a handkerchief; in comparison, those of a human are about the size of a postage stamp. This large area ensures that even the tiniest amount of scent is captured.

Soft palate

Scent-detecting receptors – the average dog has around 200 million in his nose, compared to around 5 million in a human. Scent is converted into chemical messages and transmitted to the olfactory bulb region of the brain.

Vomeronasal organ – enables your dog to identify **pheromones** (chemical substances which will be recognized by other dogs and which can influence behaviour). This information is accessed by drawing air into the mouth rather than the nose and is transmitted directly to the **limbic system**, which is the part of the brain involved with emotions.

Nostrils – a damp nose and moist nasal membranes help capture and dissolve scent molecules drawn in by taking a deep sniff.

Scent-marking

Dogs use scent to identify individuals and provide information about their sex, health and status; it is also a way in which they mark out their territory. When walking your dog, you'll notice how he carefully checks out areas that have been urine-marked by other dogs, and then often proceeds to mark over or near to them himself. Cocking a leg against a vertical surface enables him to leave his mark at nose level, where the scent will travel better through the air and be more noticeable to other dogs. Un-neutered male dogs are the most likely to scent-mark, but bitches will also sometimes do it, particularly if coming into season when it becomes a way of advertising their availability.

Another way in which your dog leaves scent 'messages' is when he passes a stool – the muscles around the anus squeeze out a few drops of a smelly secretion from the anal glands on either side. Sometimes these glands become blocked, causing discomfort, and in some cases may become infected (see page 119).

Urine-marking is one of the ways in which dogs leave scent 'messages' for each other.

Comforting smells

Because smell is so important to dogs, we can use it as a means of reassurance. A T-shirt that smells of you will comfort him if he has to stay in kennels or at the vet, while products containing a synthetic copy of pheromones produced by lactating bitches can be calming and reduce stress.

HEARING AND THE EARS

Your dog is better than you at identifying the source of a sound over greater distances, and he can hear much higher and lower frequencies. He can also differentiate between similar noises and tell whether the footsteps outside the door or the car pulling up outside the house belong to you or to someone else.

How your dog hears

Auditory ossicles – vibration of three tiny bones, also known as the hammer, anvil and stirrup, sets up waves in the fluid of the cochlea.

Semicircular canals – the other function of the ears is balance. Movement of fluid within the semicircular canals allows the brain to detect which way and how much the head is turning.

Auditory nerve – transmits nerve impulses received from the cochlea to the brain.

Pinna – the outer part of the ear catches soundwaves and directs them down the ear canal towards the eardrum.

Cochlea – change in pressure causes movement of hair cells connected to the auditory nerve and triggers nerve impulses to the auditory nerve.

Eardrum – vibrates and conducts the sound along the auditory ossicles.

Ear shapes

Upright ears are better at locating sounds than floppy ones.

- Ears come in all shapes and sizes but curved upright ears are better at detecting sounds than floppy ones. Dogs are able to hear a noise at 80 metres that you cannot hear beyond 20 metres. They can also differentiate between two notes that differ by only one-eighth of a tone.
- Independently mobile ears make it easier to pinpoint the direction from which a sound is coming – your dog can identify the location in 0.06 seconds.
- Ear shape and appearance can affect health as well as hearing ability. Floppy ears are more prone to ear infections (see page 109), while those with a lot of hair inside can trap grass seeds, which then work their way down into the ear canal.

Hearing problems

More than 80 breeds have been identified as suffering from congenital (from birth) deafness, including the Dalmatian, English Setter, white Boxers and white English Bull Terriers. Brainstem Auditory Evoked Response (BAER) diagnostic tests can be used to determine the hearing levels of adult dogs and the puppies of breeds known to be prone to this problem.

Sounds that you can't hear

Your dog can't hear as well as a cat, but he can hear sound frequencies up to 45 kHz, which enables him to discern the high-pitched noises made by small rodents, such as mice and rats, which would have formed part of his diet in the past when he still had to hunt for his food.

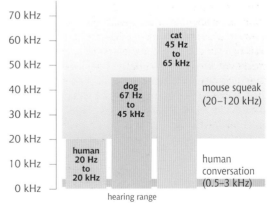

hearing range

Record-breaking ears

The longest canine ears in the world belong to Tigger, a Bloodhound from St Joseph, Illinois, and measure 34.9 cm (right ear) and 34.2 cm (left ear).

SIGHT

Human and canine eyes work in the same way, but there are a few differences in how we see the world around us. Dogs can't see the broad spectrum of colours that we do, or focus as accurately on detail. But because they evolved from hunters active at dawn and dusk, they do have a wide field of peripheral vision, are good at spotting movement and can see far better than us in dim light conditions.

How your dog sees

Eyelids and lashes – help reduce glare from sunshine and protect the eye from foreign bodies. A continual film of tears keeps the eye moist, fights infection and ensures clear vision. Excess tears collect in the corner of each eye and drain through the **nasolacrimal** duct into the nasal cavity.

Cornea – light passes through this protective layer and is directed towards the pupil and iris.

Pupil – the opening in the centre of the iris. The wider the pupil, the more light that can reach the lens.

Iris – the coloured part of the eye which expands or contracts to allow the right amount of light through the pupil.

Tapetum lucidum – this acts as a mirror, amplifying and reflecting any missed light back on to the retina for a second time.

Retina – this light-sensitive layer of cells at the back of the eye translates energy from the lightwaves into nerve impulses that are sent to the optic nerve.

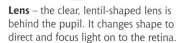

Lens – the clear, lentil-shaped lens is behind the pupil. It changes shape to direct and focus light on to the retina.

Optic nerve – transmits all gathered information to the visual centres of the brain, where it is decoded, allowing your dog to make sense of the visual world.

Your dog can see better in the dark than you

Your dog cannot see in total darkness, but is able to see better than you in low light. This is due to a combination of large pupils, the presence of a number of light-gathering cells (called rods) and a reflective membrane behind the retina. This membrane is what causes your dog's eyes to shine green in the dark when you point a torch towards him.

Dogs can see far better (left) in dim light than humans can (right).

Your dog can't see colour as well as you

Your dog can see colours, but in a much more muted range than you can; this is because good night vision is more important, so he has more light-sensitive rods than colour-sensitive cells (called cones) in his retina. Dogs are red–green colour blind and see the world in shades of blue, yellow and grey.

Dogs can see in colour, but in a more muted range (right) than we do (left).

Your dog has better peripheral vision than you

Variation in skull shape between different breeds changes eye placement and consequently field of vision.

Dogs with narrower, more tapering heads and long noses (such as Greyhounds) have eyes set farther to the side and a wide field of peripheral vision – up to 270 degrees. Long noses also obscure what can be seen just in front of the nose – which explains why a dog will sometimes apparently fail to notice a toy he is looking for which is right in front of him.

Dogs with rounder skulls and short noses (such as Pugs) have eyes that are

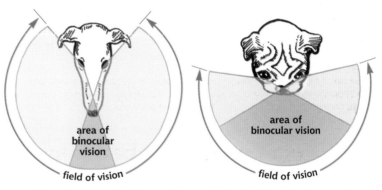

positioned more to the front, so have peripheral vision of only around 200 degrees. Eyes that are more forward-facing have better binocular vision, however, which helps in gauging distances.

Your dog sees movement better than detail

Your dog is very good at spotting movement anywhere within his range of vision, but is less able to see detail; he needs to be around 6 metres away from an object to see it as clearly as you can at 23 metres.

Stationary objects are also less easy for him to recognize than moving ones, which is why he may not be able to identify you from a distance unless you move in a characteristic way or he hears a distinctive footfall or the sound of your voice. This is also why he may run straight past a rabbit or other animal he would normally chase, without apparently noticing it, if it remains absolutely still – provided, of course, that he doesn't smell or hear it.

Your dog has three eyelids

Dogs have a third eyelid positioned behind the upper and lower outer eyelids. It moves across from the side, acting as a kind of windscreen wiper, lubricating and clearing dust from the eye. It is usually visible only for a moment as your dog opens and closes his eyes. If it becomes permanently visible it can be a sign of illness.

The third eyelid, or 'haw', is located In the inner corner of the eye and moves sideways rather than up and down.

TOUCH

Touch is a powerful but often underrated sense. It is a vital one for puppies, as it enables them to locate their mother while their eyes are still shut, and plays an important part in the development of normal emotional and social behaviour. Touch receptors are present throughout the skin; the most refined involve the 'feeler' whiskers on the face, but the pads of the feet also carry a lot of information about the environment.

Touch sensors

Different sensory receptors within the skin register pain, body movement and position, temperature, and chemical stimulation. The most numerous receptors are those that sense pressure. Located at the base of hair follicles, they are activated whenever disturbance of the hair causes movement in the surrounding tissue. The nose and muzzle are particularly rich in sensory receptors, and around 40 per cent of the area in the brain that processes all sensory information is dedicated to information received from the head, particularly the upper face and jaw.

SENSORY HAIRS

Special sensory hairs called **vibrissae** are found on your dog's head as whiskers on the eyebrows, chin and sides of the face. These stiff hairs are embedded three times more deeply than other hairs and are twice as thick. They can amplify the most subtle of touches – they are even capable of detecting vibration and sensing changes in air currents.

Never trim your dog's whiskers as they are important sensory hairs.

Pain perception

Dogs experience discomfort in a similar way to humans and, like us, perception varies between individuals, so some have higher pain thresholds than others. As well as producing physical symptoms – such as limping if a paw is injured – pain can also lead to changes in behaviour (see page 109).

Petting your dog can be a mutually pleasurable activity.

Petting your dog

Most dogs enjoy being petted and often have favourite places where they like to be stroked or gently scratched. Touching – and being touched – by your dog is a way of affirming and cementing your relationship with each other.

As well as being pleasurable, studies have shown that petting a distressed dog can also have a calming effect on him and help reduce his heart rate – and it's an activity of benefit to us as well. Hospital patients respond better to treatment and get better faster when in contact with dogs and other therapy animals, and dog owners tend to have better health generally, with lower blood cholesterol levels and fewer visits to the doctor.

Teach your dog through touch

Tellington-Touch is a teaching method that utilizes to the full the power of touch. A core part of it is a series of 'T Touches'. These special ways of touching dogs all over their bodies have been shown to improve circulation, release tension, increase confidence and deepen the bond between pet and owner. The method works on the nervous system, helping promote mental, physical and emotional balance, and bringing an enhanced ability to learn and cooperate by opening new channels of communication.

Does your dog have a sixth sense?

There are many stories about dogs exhibiting powers of telepathy, clairvoyance and precognition, but it's most likely that such tales owe more to well-developed canine senses than to possession of any psychic abilities.

HOW YOUR DOG COMMUNICATES

Dogs communicate in a variety of ways – through scent and vocalization, and by using the whole of their bodies to express themselves. Early socialization is important in teaching them how to interpret what other dogs are 'saying', as well as for learning polite and correct interaction.

Scent

Dogs use urine and stools to leave scent 'markers' notifying others of their presence, and will also spend time examining those left by other dogs (see page 36). When they meet they use their noses to find out more about each other, sniffing mouth, ears and genitals.

Vocalization

Although dogs can produce a number of different noises, canine vocabulary is limited in comparison to ours. Sounds include:

Growling – may indicate aggression, but can also invite play, depending upon tone and accompanying body language.

Howling – designed to carry over long distances, to call to another dog or to an owner when left alone. Some dogs will also howl in response to certain sounds, such as music (though no one quite knows why).

Whining – used when the dog wants something, whether food, attention, to play or to go out to relieve himself.

Whimpering/yelping – usually an indication of pain.

Barking – may be a warning, a threat or a demand for attention, or it may be due to excitement, fear or frustration. Excessive barking is more likely to occur in smaller dogs, such as Terriers and Toys; it can also be an indication of stress and boredom in dogs suffering from separation anxiety (see page 106).

Body language

Just as a single word in our language can convey different meanings depending upon context and intonation, so can each movement of your dog's body. Body language can be very subtle and complex, and dogs are generally much better at 'reading' it than we are; consequently many people have been bitten by a dog with a wagging tail, having incorrectly interpreted it as indicating happiness. A wagging tail, however, can express a whole range of emotions (see page 43), depending on tail height, tension and the speed at which it is being wagged. The more time you spend observing dogs and how they interact with each other, the better you will become at 'reading' their body language.

Communication breakdowns

Dogs are fairly good at interpreting each other's posture, but sometimes difficulties arise in understanding or indicating intention. Large amounts of facial hair or skin folds can create confusion, as can cropped ears and docked tails – although happily both these practices are now illegal in the UK and much of Europe. Dark-coloured dogs may also be harder for others to 'read', as it is more difficult to discern facial expressions.

Good socialization is important if dogs are to be able to understand and communicate their intentions clearly to each other.

Understanding your dog's body language

The following descriptions of common body-language signals used by dogs are only broad guidelines, as they can have more than one meaning. When studying your dog, it is essential to consider them within the context of what the rest of the body is doing, rather than in isolation.

Ears

Pricked:
alert, interested

Drawn back:
apprehensive, uncertain, defensive, fearful

Flattened:
fearful, threatening

Eyes

Hard, staring, unblinking:
threatening

Soft:
relaxed, contented

Half-closed:
submissive, appeasing, tired

White rim showing:
excited, stressed, fearful, in pain

Dilated pupils:
happy, excited, frightened, aroused

Face and head

Tilting head:
listening, curious

Averting gaze:
avoiding conflict, deferential

Furrowed forehead:
anxiety, concentration, puzzlement

Mouth

Licking, or quick tongue flick:
uncertain, appeasing, nervous

Yawning:
stressed, confused, pacifying

Showing teeth with lips curled up:
defensive, warning, defiant, threatening

Tight and pinched:
stressed, threatening

Relaxed, slightly open:
happy, contented

Tail

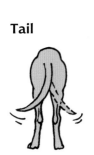
Loose, wide wag: happy, pleased, expectant

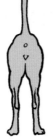
High tail: confident, curious, aggressive

Low tail: submissive, fearful, uncomfortable, uncertain

Low, frantically fast-wagging tail: anxious

Tail tucked between back legs: fearful, anxious, uncomfortable

Tail wags

A recent study revealed that when dogs felt anxious, their tails wagged more to the left. When shown something familiar or with pleasant associations, their tails wagged more to the right.

Play-bow

- Front legs extended.
- Chest lowered to ground.
- Ears back.
- Barking.
- Rump in air.
- Tail up and wagging.

Submissive

- Tail low and wagging.
- Averting gaze.
- Belly close to ground.
- Lifting paw.
- Urinating.

Threatening

- Lips drawn back, showing teeth.
- Tail high.
- Standing tall, legs stiff and straight.
- Hackles up.
- Staring, direct eye contact.

Fearful

- Tail tucked between back legs.
- Hindquarters low.
- Rounded back.
- Anxious expression.

Greeting a strange dog

Dogs observe our body language as closely as that of each other, and if you aren't careful you can inadvertently send a dog all the wrong signals about your intentions. Be particularly cautious if approaching a dog you don't know well.

Do:
- Ask the owner before you touch; some dogs may act defensively towards strangers.
- Walk towards the dog from the side; moving directly towards him from the front may be interpreted as threatening.
- Stop a metre or two before you reach him.
- Turn your head slightly. Avoid making direct eye contact or staring, as this is a confrontational action.
- Speak to the dog, using a friendly, conversational tone.
- Allow the dog to approach you and check you out by sniffing you.
- Offer the back of your hand for him to sniff, with the fingers curled into a lightly clenched fist, before you attempt to stroke him.
- Keep your movements slow and quiet, stroke gently under the throat and on the front of the chest. Patting and ruffling the fur can be uncomfortable for some dogs, and may even be considered threatening.

Don't:
- Speak in a loud or high-pitched, squeaky voice.
- Loom over the dog. If he's small and you need to get lower, bend your knees and squat, keeping your head and upper body upright.
- Cut off escape routes. If he feels concerned about you and can't move away because he's backed into a corner or on a short leash, he may become defensive.
- Ignore warning signals that he is feeling anxious about you. Move away and don't force your attentions on him.
- Greet a dog if the owner tells you he's not friendly, or if he appears to be ignoring you or trying to move away.
- Try to pet a dog left unattended outside a store or in a car.
- Attempt to kiss a dog's face.

Chapter 3

CARING FOR YOUR DOG

A dog can be more expensive to keep than you might imagine; even one as small as a Jack Russell can cost in the region of £1,000 a year.

But owning a dog isn't just about financial expenditure – it's also about being prepared to spend time caring for him. Dogs are high-maintenance pets and depend on us for absolutely everything necessary for their physical and emotional well-being, including food, shelter, exercise, veterinary care, company and affection.

Do not underestimate the amount of time and physical effort needed to keep a dog fit and happy. He will notice if you aren't around and he cannot be left to his own devices for too long if you are busy. You will need to be prepared to care for him properly every single day for many years to come.

The good news is that most dog owners feel that the pleasure and unconditional love given by their pets are worth every penny and minute spent on them. But be warned: should you fail to fulfil your dog's needs, he may become ill or unhappy, and may develop behaviour problems that can, in turn, make your life equally miserable.

GETTING READY FOR YOUR NEW DOG

There are several things you can do in advance of collecting your puppy or dog to help him settle quickly into his new home.

House rules

Before your new pet arrives, discuss and agree house rules with all members of your household. Consistent handling and treatment will prevent your dog becoming confused; it will also help him learn where he fits into the social structure of your family. Pin these rules up somewhere prominent. Points you might include are:

- Which rooms he will be allowed in and which are 'off limits'.
- Whether he is to be allowed on the furniture. If he is, this should only be when he is invited.
- No feeding scraps from the table.
- Dog not to be allowed in the kitchen while food is being prepared or cooked.
- No shouting at the dog.
- No physical punishment of the dog.
- All training to be positive and reward-based.
- Everyone to keep the house tidy so nothing is left lying around to chew on.

Familiar scents

If possible, visit your new puppy or dog several times before the day you are due to bring him home. This will allow you to get better acquainted, and a familiar person will help him feel more relaxed in his new environment.

Leaving with him an old T-shirt or blanket which smells of you will also help. If he's a puppy, by the time you collect it with him your scent will be masked by that of his littermates, and this will comfort him on his first few nights away from them.

Everyone in the house needs to agree on any areas that are 'off limits' for your dog.

Caring for your dog

Choosing a name

Choose a name that is easy for you to call and for your dog to recognize. One or two syllables tend to work best, but avoid names that sound similar to verbal cues you'll be using when training – such as 'Kit', which he will find difficult to distinguish from 'Sit'. Try to choose a name before you collect your puppy, then you can ask the breeder to use it with him. If you wait too long to decide, there's a danger that he'll start responding to 'puppy' instead!

If you are adopting a rescue dog he may already have a name. However, some owners like to give a new name in recognition of a fresh start in life, in which case he will need to be taught to respond to it (see page 84).

Your dog's sense of smell can be used to help him settle in his new home.

Comforting pheromones

Dog Appeasing Pheromone (DAP) is a natural chemical produced by bitches soon after giving birth. It emits a message of reassurance and safety and has been developed in a commercially available synthetic form which can be bought from your vet. It can help both puppies and older dogs feel less stressed by new surroundings.

A DAP diffuser works like a plug-in air freshener, constantly releasing the pheromone. If possible install it the day before you collect your dog to enable levels to build up. Put it near floor level so he can sit next to it if he wants.

The product is also available as a spray, which can be used before car journeys, or on a bandanna around his neck to help him feel calm and secure when he is in a situation that may cause him anxiety.

THE FIRST FEW WEEKS

The first few weeks with your new puppy or dog will probably seem pretty hectic to both of you as you spend time getting used to each other and to the changes in your accustomed routines. But even before you collect your new charge you are likely to find yourself busier than usual as you get ready for his arrival.

Shopping for your new dog

Although some of the basic essentials you'll need for your new puppy or dog are one-off expenses, many of them (such as food and insurance) will be ongoing, while other items will need replacing as they become outgrown or suffer wear and tear. Everything here should be available from a good pet shop. You can also buy online but there can be a bewildering amount of choice, so if you are uncertain about which products will be best for your pet, visit a shop to obtain advice.

Food – buy the brand and type that your puppy or dog is already used to in order to avoid tummy upsets. See also pages 61–64.

Treats – select those suitable to use as training rewards (see also page 79), and others that are longer lasting to help clean and exercise teeth and gums and to satisfy chewing urges.

Food and water bowls – choose steel or ceramic rather than plastic if your new dog is likely to chew. The extra weight of a ceramic water bowl means it is less likely to be overturned. See also page 63.

Bed – initially, a cut-down cardboard box will be fine for a small puppy, but once he's outgrown it he will need a proper bed. Avoid wicker, foam or beanbag types until he is past the chewing stages – aside from the mess if he takes them apart, they could be dangerous if ingested. The rigid plastic variety is more durable and easy to clean. It can be made cosy with blankets or Vetbed, a soft fleecy bedding that is easy to wash and non-allergenic.

Collar and leash – you will need to buy new ones as he grows or if they become worn. Use only flat collars, made of nylon web, cotton web or leather. Never use a choke chain. For more information, see page 79. You should also get an ID tag engraved with your details to attach to his collar (see page 73).

First aid kit – you can buy a ready-made one from pet shops or make up your own (see page 114).

46

Poop bags – plus a poop-scoop if you wish. Baby nappy bags can be cheaper than those sold specifically for dogs. See pages 51 and 71.

A **'Kong'** – a rubber toy which can be stuffed with food and given to your pet to occupy him when you need to leave him on his own. See page 93.

Toys – get some to use when playing with him, others that can be chewed and a few with which he can amuse himself and which will offer mental stimulation as well as fun. Make sure they are sufficiently robust and appropriately sized for his age and breed (see page 93).

Stair-gate – this will prevent access to areas you want to keep out of bounds or which might prove hazardous, such as stairways. You may be able to buy one cheaply second-hand.

Crate – this will offer a safe den and can also be used for him to travel in the car or at times when you can't supervise him at home (see page 60).

Stain and odour remover – use a type specially formulated for pet stains and smells, as this will be both safe for your pet and effective.

Anti-chew spray – particularly useful with a puppy during the chewing stages to prevent him damaging things or harming himself.

Grooming kit – a soft brush or grooming mitt will probably be sufficient for puppies. Once the adult coat begins to grow through, buy more tools appropriate for his coat type (see page 65). Nail clippers will prevent his nails becoming overlong (see page 67).

Insurance

Take this out as soon as you buy your dog. Use Yellow Pages or the internet to research insurance companies and look carefully at the different sorts of policy they offer. When contacting an insurer, be honest about any existing health issues that your new dog has. For more information on insurance, see page 121.

Preparing your house

Curiosity about his new surroundings can get your dog into big trouble. Going down on your hands and knees will give you a similar perspective to his and make it easier for you to spot potential hazards.

Electrical cables should be enclosed where possible or tidied out of reach so that they can't be chewed. If necessary use an anti-chew spray – it may need topping up frequently.

Cupboards containing medications, cleaning materials and food should be securely closed. If necessary fit childproof locks. Ensure rubbish bins can't be opened.

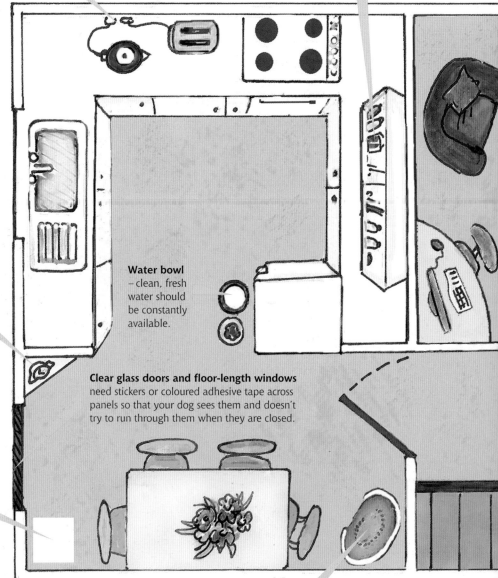

Ornaments – put anything breakable safely out of reach of both teeth and wagging tails.

Water bowl – clean, fresh water should be constantly available.

Clear glass doors and floor-length windows need stickers or coloured adhesive tape across panels so that your dog sees them and doesn't try to run through them when they are closed.

Toilet area – if you live in an apartment without easy access to the outdoors you may wish to choose an area inside where it is acceptable for your dog to relieve himself. Choose somewhere easy to clean and use commercially produced toilet pads (see page 60).

Bed – make his bed cosy and inviting. Position it out of draughts and where he won't be disturbed by people walking past when he wants to sleep.

Fires – whether electric, gas or real, use a fireguard to keep dogs at a safe distance. Many dogs love to bake themselves in front of the fire and will get as close as they can.

Tidy up – don't leave food on plates, put away all toys and keep items like TV remote controls out of reach.

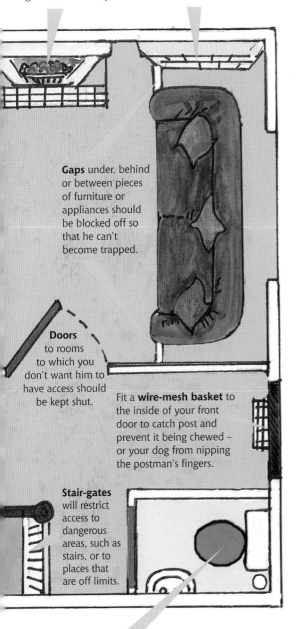

Gaps under, behind or between pieces of furniture or appliances should be blocked off so that he can't become trapped.

Doors to rooms to which you don't want him to have access should be kept shut.

Fit a **wire-mesh basket** to the inside of your front door to catch post and prevent it being chewed – or your dog from nipping the postman's fingers.

Stair-gates will restrict access to dangerous areas, such as stairs, or to places that are off limits.

Toilet – cleaning chemicals could be harmful so make sure the lid is kept down to prevent your dog drinking from the bowl.

DOORS AND WINDOWS

Teach your pet to sit and wait for permission to go through the front door (see page 105). This will prevent him from escaping and possibly becoming lost or involved in a road accident. For advice on doors with large glass panels and floor-length windows, see diagram.

HOUSE PLANTS

Place any house plants where they can't be chewed and where your dog won't be tempted to dig in the soil. The following common house plants can be toxic to your dog – make sure that any you have are out of reach. If you have nowhere safe to put them, give them away or safely dispose of them.

- African Violet
- Amaryllis
- Cyclamen
- Dracaena
- Dumb Cane
- Kalanchoe
- Mother-in-law's Tongue
- Philodendron
- Poinsettia
- Rubber Plant
- Umbrella Plant

Christmas

Christmas can be full of hazards for pets. Keep your dog out of a room with a Christmas tree unless you are there to ensure he doesn't try to play with the decorations or to unwrap any presents left beneath it. Vacuum frequently to help prevent pine needles becoming trapped in his paws.

Seasonal plants – poinsettias, holly, ivy and mistletoe – can be toxic if eaten, as can chocolate (see page 62).

The bangs made by crackers can be frightening to animals, so either put your dog in another room while they are being pulled or remove the snaps first. Celebratory fireworks may also scare him. See page 102 for advice on helping your dog cope with loud noises.

A dog-friendly garden

It is possible to create a pleasant outdoor space for you and your dog to enjoy, but you may need to make a few changes in order to make it escape-proof and ensure that it provides a safe environment.

Gates – make sure that puppies and small dogs can't wriggle under any gap at the bottom. They should be too high to be jumped over, and catches should work properly so that they can't be nudged open. If the gate is used by the postman and other callers, always check that it has been properly secured before letting your dog into the garden.

Mulches – do not use cocoa-shell mulches on flowerbeds: dogs find the chocolate smell highly attractive but it can be fatal if ingested. Use untreated bark chips, or even large pebbles, which will also discourage your dog from walking over the bed as he will dislike the feel.

Electrical cables should be securely enclosed so they cannot be chewed.

Plant containers – if your dog is liable to chew the tops of plastic tubs, replace them with containers made of stone, metal or terracotta. The taller the pot the better if you have a male dog who is likely to cock a leg against them, as urine will run down the side instead of soaking into the compost. If need be, increase height by raising the pot on bricks.

Ponds and swimming pools should be fenced off to prevent access. Water-loving dogs may enjoy a paddling pool in warm weather. Buy one made from rigid plastic and always supervise its use.

Plants – remove any that are poisonous; dogs often lack caution when choosing what to graze on.

Toilet area – it may be useful to train your dog to use a particular area of the garden. If you wish, you could also install a 'dog loo' (see page 51).

Digging area – a dog who loves to dig can quickly ruin your garden, disturbing plants and leaving craters in the lawn. Provide an outlet for this urge by building a sandbox (see page 51) so you can confine digging activities to one area of the garden.

Young children – if possible, fence off a separate 'people only' spot where your children can play but your dog isn't allowed.

Garden chemicals – always follow the instructions if using sprays or dusts and be particularly wary of pellets which are likely to be toxic for dogs as well as pests. See *The Green Garden Expert* for organic alternatives.

Boundaries – a wooden or wire fence or a wall is essential to secure your garden properly, as a determined dog will push through even the prickliest of hedges. It may be necessary to sink the bottom of the fence below ground level, or to pave or concrete along the edge to deter digging. It should be high enough to discourage any attempt to jump out. Small dogs can manage a surprising height – ask the breeder's advice if unsure.

Storage – keep tools safely in a shed or tool store. Keep your dog indoors when operating machinery such as lawnmowers and hedge trimmers.

Shady areas will be appreciated in warm weather, although some dogs don't know when they have had enough sun and may need to be taken indoors during the hottest parts of the day.

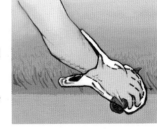

POOP SCOOPING

Pick up any faeces from the garden each day; leaving it poses a health hazard to you and your dog. There are several ways in which you can dispose of it, depending on the size of your garden and your personal preferences:

- Install a 'dog loo' – a special container that is buried in the garden, and to which you regularly add an activator to help break down the waste.
- Flush it down your toilet. You can buy special flushable bags to make this easier.
- Buy a system designed to fit on to your outdoor soil pipe into which you can dispose of faeces.
- Bury it.
- Invest in a wormery, but ensure the worms are the sort that feed exclusively on animal waste, not the sort that live on kitchen waste.
- Take it to your nearest public dog-waste bin.
- If absolutely necessary, *small* amounts can be disposed of, double-bagged, in ordinary litter bins or with your household waste. Do *not* put it on compost heaps or in green-waste bins.

POISONOUS PLANTS

Be careful about which plants you have in your garden; dogs use their mouths to help them find out about their environment and often also enjoy browsing herbage. The following are some of the most common poisonous garden plants – you can find a more comprehensive list on the Dogs Trust website (see page 126).

- Azalea
- Baby's Breath
- Bleeding Heart Plant
- Bluebell
- Box
- Christmas Rose
- Crocus
- Foxglove
- Geranium
- Hibiscus
- Ivy
- Lupin
- Snowdrop
- Sweet Pea
- Tobacco Plant
- Wisteria
- Yarrow
- Yew

SANDBOX

Some breeds love to dig, and building a sandbox provides the opportunity to do so without spoiling the whole garden. It is simple to build one, and you can encourage your dog to focus on this particular area of the garden. Keep it interesting for him by burying special 'treasures' such as toys and chewy treats for him to discover.

Barbecues

If you are having a barbecue it's safer not to allow your dog to join in. Keep him inside, away from the hot cooking area and the temptation of unsuitable food, as well as the dangers of discarded skewers.

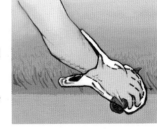

Caring for your dog

51

Children and dogs

Dogs can be a wonderful addition to a family. As well as being playmates, they help teach children patience, tolerance, kindness and a sense of responsibility. Research also shows that children who grow up with pets – particularly dogs – from an early age tend to be more confident, make friends more easily and are better adjusted socially than those who don't.

GETTING ALONG TOGETHER

Children need to be taught that dogs are not toys and should be encouraged to treat them with respect. For the safety and well-being of both, spend time talking to your children about how they can help the new dog or puppy settle in and become a happy member of the family.

Smaller children should be shown how to stroke and pet the dog, using a cuddly toy to demonstrate with and practise on. Explain that patting doesn't feel very nice to the dog and show them how to stroke gently along the neck, chest and back instead. This can also be a good time to teach them about the signals a dog may use to indicate that he is feeling uncomfortable or unhappy with what the child is doing, and how he might react if they persist.

ADDITIONAL HOUSE RULES

If you have children, you'll need to expand your list of house rules: make sure all adults abide by them as well to set a good example. Especially with younger children, it helps if you go through each of the following points, explaining how they will help the dog to be happy and better behaved, and the child to be safe:

- Wash hands after playing with or handling the dog and before eating.
- No sharing plates of food.
- No touching the dog when he is sleeping.
- Leave the dog alone when he is eating.
- Play gently – no rough games or encouraging the dog to jump up.
- No teasing.
- Don't share toys with the dog; if he steals one, ask an adult to help get it back.
- No chasing the dog.
- No picking the dog up in case he is squeezed too tightly or is dropped.
- No hitting, kicking, smacking or screaming at the dog.

No matter how well behaved your dog or child is, never leave them together unsupervised.

Take time to explain to children why some behaviours shouldn't be encouraged.

LETTING YOUR CHILDREN HELP

It's natural that children will want to join in doing things with the dog. This is to be encouraged. It will help your dog to learn his place within the family and build bonds with all its members.

How much children are able to participate in caring for the dog depends on their age, but involve them as much as possible in chores such as feeding, grooming, checking and filling water bowls, as well as going for walks, playing with and petting the dog. If you have more than one child, draw up a rota so that everyone gets a chance to do the more enjoyable things and takes a turn at those which are less so. This will also ensure that the dog doesn't become either the centre of disputes or overwhelmed with attention.

Children can also become involved in training, which will help foster mutual respect and develop handling skills. The whole family can attend training classes – some clubs also have junior sections designed for younger handlers.

Safety

In all interaction between children and dogs, safety considerations must be paramount. Recent years have seen a substantial rise in the number of people in both the UK and the USA taken to hospital as a result of dog bites. Of these, 50 per cent are children, with the average age being 15. Research into dog attacks reveals that by the age of 14 more than half of all children in the UK have been bitten by a dog. It should also be remembered that most dog attacks occur at home or in a familiar place.

Leaving a child or young teenager alone with a dog carries considerable risks. Young children may fail to recognize warning signs or be unable to interpret them correctly, and they can sometimes be unintentionally cruel or excessively rough. Older children may get into trouble through complacency caused by over-familiarity. Puppies and younger dogs can also become over-exuberant and inadvertently cause injury as a result.

- If your child has friends round, take your dog to another room so that he doesn't become over-excited by any boisterous play. Although you may have spent time teaching your own children how to behave around dogs, other parents may not have taught theirs!
- For their own safety and that of the animal, no child should be allowed to walk a dog without adult supervision unless you are certain that they have proper control.
- Children who have become confident around dogs through having their own will also need to be discouraged from rushing up to other dogs that they see. Explain that not all dogs like strangers. Teach them to ask the owner for permission to approach and, if this is given, to introduce themselves to the dog correctly (see page 43).

New baby

If you are expecting a baby and already have a dog, there will be lots of changes for both of you to cope with, so spend some time preparing him.

BEFORE THE BABY ARRIVES

- Make sure all vaccinations, flea and worming treatments are up to date.
- If your dog has any behaviour or jealousy issues, consult a behavioural counsellor or trainer.
- Make sure training is up to scratch and that your dog will settle down on command.
- Introduce any changes to routine so that he is accustomed to being walked and fed at different times or in different places or by different people.
- Leave buggies and cradles around the house so that they become familiar objects. If planning to walk your dog while pushing a pram or baby buggy, start doing it now to get him used to it and to going at a slower pace.
- Set up baby-gates at places where your dog will not be allowed. Start excluding him from those places if he's been allowed there previously.
- Play CDs of baby noises.
- Buy a doll, cuddle and talk to it and pretend to change it in your dog's presence. Praise and reward him for quiet, good behaviour.
- Buy some new toys to give to your dog while you are doing things with the baby.

AFTER THE BIRTH

- Ask someone to take home an item of clothing or a blanket the baby has been wrapped in so that the baby's scent becomes familiar to your dog.
- When you return home, ask someone else to hold the baby so that you can greet your dog with empty arms. When you introduce the baby, put your dog's leash on so that you can control his movements, then ask him to sit next to the person holding the baby. Allow him to sniff the baby, but not to touch.
- Try to keep to the new routine you've devised as much as possible and make time to play with your dog and give him attention. Create positive associations with the baby's presence by giving him special treats and toys.
- Never leave the baby unattended with the dog.

Never take liberties with your dog's good nature by placing him in a situation he may find difficult to cope with.

> **TIP** Babies are tiring; don't get a new puppy or dog if you are expecting – you may not have time or energy for both. Wait till you have a settled routine and feel on top of things before taking on another responsibility.

The first day

Bringing a new puppy or dog home is an exciting event for you, but it can be an unsettling one for the new arrival. The transition will be easier for him if you have been able to visit him a few times before collecting him, but you can also make the first day in his new home easier for him to cope with by being well organized.

COLLECTING YOUR PUPPY OR DOG

Arrive early so that your puppy or dog has as much of the day as possible in which to get used to his new surroundings. He will then also be more likely to settle at bedtime.

Getting him home

The safest way for your pet to travel if he is a puppy or small dog is in a well-ventilated plastic pet carrier. Line it with comfortable bedding and secure it on the back seat of your car using a seatbelt restraint so that it doesn't slide around. A larger dog should travel in a crate or behind a dog guard so that he can't interfere with or distract the driver. Leave a leash on so that when you open the car door it is easy to hold on to him and prevent any risk of him running off.

ARRIVING HOME

Take your pup or dog outside immediately so that he can relieve himself, after which you can show him his bed and water bowl. A puppy may feel tired after the journey and be ready for a nap. If so, let him sleep and then take him straight out to relieve himself again as soon as he wakes.

Ask friends to wait a few days before coming to see him so that he has a chance to settle in first.

A pet carrier is the safest way to transport a puppy or small dog home.

Exploring

For the rest of the day and those following, allow him to begin exploring his new environment. Keep a watchful eye on him to ensure he doesn't come to harm, and spend time playing, handling and getting to know him. If he has had his full course of vaccinations (see page 111) he can accompany you on walks, but do not allow him to run off-leash until you have first taught him a good recall (see page 91).

On arriving home, take your puppy straight out to the garden to relieve himself.

What you should receive when you collect your puppy

As well as the puppy, you should also be given:

- A written receipt giving his particulars, including price.
- Details of his worming programme – product used, when given and date of next treatment.
- A vaccination certificate if he has had his first injection.
- A diet sheet containing details of what, when and how much he is currently eating.
- Pedigree and registration documents – these should be originals, not photocopies. Check they are all in order and that any sections the breeder needs to sign for you to register change of ownership have been completed.
- Certification relating to any screening tests.
- A few weeks' free insurance may be included.

Many breeders will also send you off with a whole sheaf of information on general puppy care.

Dogs from rescue shelters should be accompanied by details of vaccination, worming, diet and, if applicable, microchipping (see page 72).

Supervise your puppy as he explores his new surroundings and spend some time interacting with him.

FEEDING

Stick to the diet and feeding times to which your dog or puppy is accustomed to help the settling-in process. Sudden changes, especially when combined with the stress and excitement of being in a new place, can result in stomach upsets. If you want to change anything, wait a fortnight and then gradually introduce any alterations over the space of the next week.

THE FIRST NIGHT

A puppy may cry at night because he is lonely and afraid, missing his mother and siblings. If this happens, settle him in a crate (see page 60) in your bedroom near your bed, and if he wakes during the night don't pet him but speak soothingly to reassure him. If you suspect he is being restless because he needs to relieve himself, take him straight out, but without making a fuss of him, and bring him straight back in when he's finished.

Once he begins sleeping through the night you can begin to move the crate out. First move it to the door of your room, then just outside it but with the door open, then to the foot of the stairs, until it's finally in the place where you want him to sleep.

Your puppy may well feel lonely and anxious on the first nights he spends away from his siblings.

The next few days

Once your new puppy or dog has had a couple of days to settle in, encourage visitors to call round. Meeting new people forms an important part of his education. Invite friends in ones and twos so that he isn't too overwhelmed, and begin teaching him how to behave politely when they arrive. Ask your guests to bring 'props' with them such as umbrellas, walking sticks, hats and bags to accustom him to different appearances.

INTRODUCING NEW EXPERIENCES

Handle your new puppy every day, gradually building up the time you spend doing so. Inspect his head one day, looking in his ears, eyes, mouth and teeth, and using treats to make it a rewarding experience. On another day, feel down his legs, pick up and look at each paw, and gently take hold of his tail. Go slowly, talking to him soothingly as you do so. This will stand you in good stead in the future when doing health checks or grooming, if the vet needs to examine him or if you plan to show him. You can also:

- Start doing some gentle grooming with soft brushes, even if he still has a puppy coat that doesn't really need much attention.
- At feeding times add little bits of really tasty food to his bowl while he is eating so that he doesn't become defensive when you are close, but instead associates your presence with something pleasant.
- Gradually accustom him to the sounds of domestic appliances such as dishwashers and vacuum cleaners.
- Introduce some simple training, keeping sessions short and fun.

If you have an older rescue dog, don't assume that he will be familiar with any of these experiences, so follow a similar procedure and be just as patient with him as you would be with a puppy.

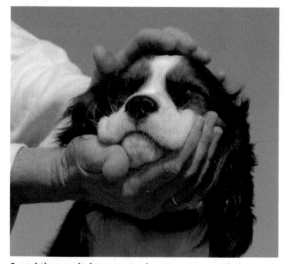

Spend time each day accustoming your puppy to being handled all over his body.

Discuss preventative health issues when you take your puppy to the vet for a health check.

ARRANGE A HEALTH CHECK

Book an appointment for the vet to give your pet a health check, to arrange for any vaccinations (see page 111), and to discuss a suitable flea and worming programme and any other issues, such as neutering (see pages 9 and 111). Take some treats with you and ask the staff at the practice to make a fuss of him so that his visit is as positive an experience as possible.

GOING OUT

Until your puppy has completed his primary course of vaccinations (see page 111), he won't be fully protected against diseases that can be transmitted by other dogs, so you will need to be careful about where you take him. You can continue getting him used to new experiences, but you need to exercise common sense. Take him on short car rides, visit friends and introduce him to dogs you know are vaccinated – do this in either their home or yours. Don't allow him to mix with other dogs of unknown vaccination status or to walk in places they may have frequented. If necessary, carry him to avoid contact.

TIP Although your puppy may seem like a whirlwind of energy at times, take care not to over-exercise him to try to tire him out. It may be tempting, but too much exercise increases the risk of joint problems.

INTRODUCING OTHER PETS

Other animals you own may not share your enthusiasm about a new arrival, so care must be taken with introductions to ensure the safety and well-being of all your pets.

Introducing dogs to dogs

Think carefully before introducing a new dog into your home if you already have one. Elderly dogs in particular may find a bouncy youngster stressful, and responses can vary from being highly intolerant to allowing merciless pestering.

- Make sure someone is available to help so you can handle one dog each. First introductions are ideally made on 'neutral' ground outdoors and away from home, but if you have a young puppy who has not yet had his final course of vaccinations, the next best place is the garden.
- Be confident, relaxed and upbeat, as any anxiety will be communicated to the dogs and each may attribute it to the presence of the other.
- Avoid a face-to-face introduction, as this can seem confrontational. It is better to walk the dogs parallel to each other in the same direction.
- When each seems happy in the other's company, allow them to sniff at and investigate each other. If they become tense or get excited, separate them, give them each a treat and repeat the earlier steps.

- Once they can accept each other's presence calmly, take them home and indoors. Make sure all beds, toys and food are removed so that there are no quarrels over them. Allow them to walk around the house together with leashes on. Gradually put bedding and toys back, one at a time.
- Supervise all interaction and separate them when you need to go out until you feel it is safe to leave them alone together. Even when they get along well, never leave them unsupervised with food. You may also need to take care with toys if one of the dogs is possessive.
- Ensure you spend quality one-to-one time with each dog.

Introducing a rescue dog

If you are getting a rescue dog, a reputable shelter will insist that your current dog meets the prospective new one before agreeing to his adoption. They will also be able to help and advise you on the introduction. Assuming all goes well, take both dogs for a walk together before taking the new one into your home for the first time, then follow the steps above.

Allow new dogs to meet resident pets on neutral ground if possible and avoid any confrontational introductions.

Introducing dogs to cats

Equal care needs to be taken when introducing dogs and cats –
each is capable of inflicting terrible injuries on the other.

Don't allow your dog to chase your cat, even in play.

Make sure that your cat has her own places where she can feel safe, such as high areas only she is agile enough to reach. Alternatively, keep one room as a special place for your cat. Leave the door shut but fit a cat flap so that she can come and go as she wishes. This also solves the problem of where to put litter trays, which can be irresistible to dogs. Make it a pleasant place for her to be, with toys, water, bedding and her food.

When making first introductions:

- If possible, arrange for another person to be on hand to help.
- Try to keep excitement and stress levels low. Don't try to rush things or force contact.
- Keep the dog on the leash so that you can control his movements. Give 'Watch me' commands (see page 84) and offer your dog tasty treats when he obeys.
- When they seem comfortable in each other's presence, allow the dog to sniff at the cat and, if all is well, remove the leash. It may take several introductory sessions before you reach this stage. If you are unsure, leave the leash on, trailing behind him, so that you can take hold of it quickly should you need to.
- Keep a watchful eye on both and leave a door open so that your cat has an escape route.

TIP If you are rehoming an adult dog from a rescue shelter, ask if staff have tested his response to cats before you bring him home to live with your own!

- If the dog dives towards or barks at the cat, don't punish him, but give a 'Leave it' command then a high-value treat when he obeys (see pages 88 and 79).
- If you think the cat may try to run during initial introductions, put her in a cat carrier rather than leaving her loose, and don't allow the dog to investigate her too closely until she has become more confident.
- Until they have got to know each other and are relaxed in each other's presence, avoid carrying the cat when your dog is loose. If the dog jumps up to investigate, the cat may panic, claw you, and your control of the situation will be lost. Remain cautious of carrying your cat at any time if you have a dog who is inclined to be jealous or a cat who is nervous.
- Never allow the dog to chase the cat, even in play.
- Avoid exciting games or creating other situations that might trigger your dog's hunting instinct if the cat is near.

Be especially careful about feeding: a cat who approaches an eating dog may get herself into deep trouble. Supervise mealtimes and never leave them alone together with food.

Fitting a cat flap to an interior door can give your cat some privacy when she wants it.

Small furry animals

Keep small furry pets, such as rabbits, mice, guinea pigs and hamsters, safely away from your dog, as their appearance and the squeaky noises they make can often trigger hunting instincts in even the most placid of dogs.

HOUSE-TRAINING

House-training should start from the moment you bring your new puppy home. If you have adopted an older dog from a rescue centre, he may not necessarily have been house-trained; even if he was, he may have lost clean habits while staying in kennels. Treat him as though he were a puppy until he learns where to go and how to ask to be let out.

TEACHING YOUR PUPPY TO BE CLEAN

Being consistent, vigilant, patient and establishing a definite routine will help your puppy learn to be clean indoors. House-training can take several weeks, sometimes longer. You shouldn't expect a dog under the age of six months to be able to control his bladder for more than a few hours during the day when he is awake and active.

Take your puppy out frequently to visit the places you want him to use as a toilet area (see also page 60). He'll need to go more frequently during the daytime. Don't pick him up and carry him, otherwise he won't learn how to go to the door and ask to go out.

Toileting is a scent-related activity, so although you shouldn't let messes build up, leaving one stool in the spot you've chosen will encourage him to use that area.

Keep him on a leash and avoid interacting with him, so that he doesn't become distracted from the reason you're both out there. Praise him lavishly when he does relieve himself and, once he's finished, reward him with a treat.

You may also like to teach a verbal cue. If you quietly say 'Empty' or whatever you prefer when your puppy is urinating or defecating, he will soon come to associate the action with the word. Later on, this will enable you to prompt him to relieve himself when you want him to – for example, before a car trip.

GOLDEN RULES

Puppies have poor bladder control when young. Your puppy will need to relieve himself:
- **First thing in the morning.**
- **Every two hours during the day – and possibly more frequently at first.**
- **Immediately after he eats or drinks.**
- **After play.**
- **After waking from a nap.**
- **Last thing at night.**
- **Every two to three hours during the night for the first few weeks.**

SIGNS THAT YOUR PUPPY MAY NEED TO RELIEVE HIMSELF

- Circling.
- Sniffing at the floor.
- Suddenly stopping in the middle of whatever he is doing.
- Whining.
- Pawing at the ground.
- Beginning to squat.

IF YOUR PUPPY HAS AN ACCIDENT INDOORS

With a puppy, it's likely that you'll have at least one 'accident' in the house, and quite likely rather more than this until he has gained better bladder control and learned how to tell you when he needs to go out. When it happens:
- Don't tell him off and **never** rub his nose in the soiled area. This may cause him to find hiding places in which to toilet.
- Take him straight out to the garden or designated toilet area.
- Clean the soiled area thoroughly with a non-ammonia-based smell- and stain-removing product so that the scent doesn't encourage him to use the same area again.

Puppies need to empty their bladders frequently: you'll soon learn to spot signs that he needs to go out.

TOILET-TRAINING DIFFICULTIES

Small breeds may take longer to become house-trained than larger ones, but if you feel you're having a lot of trouble teaching this, or if your puppy suddenly seems to have forgotten what he's learned, it could be due to:
- A health problem – take him to the vet for a check-up.
- Stress – some puppies, and some older dogs, may temporarily lose control of their bladders at times of excitement or if they feel threatened or frightened.
- Separation anxiety – often accompanied by other symptoms such as barking and destructiveness (see page 106).

Paper training

Paper training has drawbacks:

- It teaches your puppy that it is all right to relieve himself indoors. He may also have difficulty differentiating between the toilet area and the rest of your home.
- It delays the process of teaching your puppy to relieve himself outdoors.
- A change to using a toilet area outside will seem inconsistent and confusing.
- You may create a preference for paper so that he is reluctant to use any other surface.

It is best to teach your puppy to relieve himself outdoors right from the start, but if you have no quick access to a private garden it may be necessary to paper train him. Use paper puppy training pads rather than newspaper: their greater absorbency will reduce the likelihood of your puppy walking in his mess and treading it around your home. Place them in the area you want him to use: bathroom or kitchen floors are easiest to clean if he misses. Place a plastic sheet beneath and position them away from his bed and food/water dishes as he will be reluctant to soil near these. Teach him to use them in exactly the same way as when teaching him to toilet outdoors. When you eventually want to teach him to go outdoors, do so by gradually moving the pads closer to the door, and eventually to outside it.

CRATE TRAINING

A crate (or 'house kennel') can come in useful on many occasions, so it is worth spending some time introducing it to your dog and creating pleasant associations with being inside it.

WHY HAVE A CRATE?

A collapsible wire crate combines sturdiness with ease of storage, while also providing good ventilation and an all-round view for your dog. If you are staying at a hotel with your dog and need to leave him unattended for short periods, it will be a familiar environment for him and you'll know he won't be getting up to mischief. When travelling, a crate will help keep him safe and prevent him from distracting the driver. Also, if he ever needs to spend time at the vet's he will be less distressed if he's already accustomed to being in a confined space. A crate can also be used to create an area that feels safe for a dog who is scared of thunder or fireworks (see page 104). It is invaluable for a puppy, as it will keep him out of trouble when you are unable to supervise him.

INTRODUCING A CRATE

It's important that your dog thinks of his crate or playpen as a nice place to be, so create pleasant associations and take your time introducing it.

- Make it inviting by placing comfortable bedding and a few toys inside. Make sure drinking water is also available and place treats inside for him to find.
- Leave the door open at first so he can come and go as he wishes.
- Feed all meals in the crate.
- When he's tired and ready for a rest, encourage him to go into the crate with a chew toy.
- When he's confident about going in and will happily settle there, you can shut the door for short periods.

CRATE RULES

- Although it's fine to expect your dog to spend the night in his crate with the door shut, don't leave him in such a small space for extended periods during the day – no more than one hour at a time and four hours in total.
- Never use being put in the crate as a punishment; it shouldn't be somewhere you push him into when you're cross.
- Always give your dog the chance to relieve himself before putting him in his crate.
- Use the right size of crate: there should be enough room for your dog to stand up and turn around in comfortably. Allow 7.5–10 cm extra headroom when he is standing.
- Use the crate while you are at home as well as when you go out.

Make your dog's crate a place he enjoys.

PLAYPEN

If you have enough space, a playpen can provide a roomier alternative to a crate for those occasions when you can't supervise your puppy. Protect the floor beneath it with polythene and then a layer of newspaper to absorb any urine. The same rules apply as when using a crate. Introduce it in the same way; make it a nice place to be with toys, treats and a comfortable bed; and never leave your puppy in it for longer than an hour.

FEEDING YOUR DOG

Although dogs have evolved to eat a range of different foodstuffs, their diet needs to contain the right balance of protein, fat, carbohydrate, minerals and vitamins to provide them with energy and to prevent illness.

Types of food

The simplest and most convenient way to feed your dog is to buy a commercially pre-prepared food. All the hard work of preparation and working out nutritional requirements has been done for you, so all you need to do is serve it. Alternatively, you can create your own home-prepared meals, but this can be time consuming and will require plenty of research.

PRE-PREPARED FOOD

Commercial food falls into two categories, 'complete' or 'complementary' – manufacturers must state on the packaging which of these terms applies.

Complete foods are available in wet, dry or semi-moist forms and contain all the nutrients your dog needs for a balanced diet. He will not require any additional foods.

Complementary foods are those that do not provide a balanced diet on their own, but are fed in addition to other foods. Treats fall into this category, as does biscuit mixer which is added to meat. Treats should not form more than 10–15 per cent of the total diet.

Researching commercial food

Most pet-food manufacturers have websites containing more detailed information on their products than may be on the label; many also have their own helplines which you can ring if you have a query. Contact details should be displayed on the packaging.

Wet food

Sold in tins, pouches or plastic cartons in a range of flavours.

Advantages. Ready-made and easy-to-store portions which most pets find highly palatable.

Disadvantages. More expensive than dry food, as up to 70 per cent of what you pay for is moisture. Also messier.

Dry food

Dry foods are a mix of cereals and meat that has been cooked, cut into pieces and then dried. The crunchy biscuits or 'kibble' are then sprayed with minerals, vitamins, fats, oils and any other ingredients that aren't heat-tolerant. Most can be fed dry, but check the instructions as some may need rehydrating.

Advantages. More cost-effective than wet food. Hygienic, easy to feed, convenient and with no off-putting smell.

Disadvantages. Less tempting than wet foods and easy to overfeed.

Semi-moist food

As the name suggests, this falls between wet and dry foods, containing 25–35 per cent moisture.

Advantages. Highly palatable, usually available in portion-sized pouches.

Disadvantages. High salt/sugar content (used as preservatives), so not the healthiest option, and can be more expensive than wet food.

'Lifestage' and 'prescription' diets

- 'Lifestage' diets fall into three main categories – puppy, adult and senior – which aim to satisfy the changing nutritional requirements of your dog at each stage of his life. During the rapid-growth stage of his puppyhood he can need up to two and a half times as many calories per kilogram of body weight as an adult dog, plus appropriate levels of minerals and vitamins to ensure healthy development. When he reaches maturity at around 12–18 months he can change to an adult maintenance diet until ageing causes him to be less active and his digestive processes to be less efficient. A 'senior' diet takes these and other physical changes into account by containing extra antioxidants to help the immune system and added nutrients for skin and gut health. Lifestage diets are usually available as both wet and dry foods.

- Diets designed specially for small, medium, large and giant breeds, which develop at different rates, are also available. There are even several breed-specific foods on the market.
- Lifestyle, as well as lifestage, foods are also available, with 'active' or 'working' diets suitable for dogs with increased energy requirements, and 'light' foods for those inclined to put on weight.
- Special diets, available only on prescription from your vet, can help in the management or treatment of certain health problems, such as kidney, liver, heart and bowel disorders, weight loss and diabetes. If your vet prescribes a special diet, check your pet insurance, as the cost may be covered by the policy.

ALTERNATIVE FOODS

Some owners prefer to feed a raw food or home-made diet, but either of these alternatives requires research to ensure your dog's nutritional needs are met.

The BARF diet

BARF is an acronym for Biologically Appropriate Raw Food, which is based on the idea that dogs should be given as 'natural' a diet as possible, eating uncooked foods as they would in the wild. Ingredients include raw meaty bones, offal and crushed vegetables, plus supplementary foods such as cottage cheese, yogurt, small quantities of fruit, various herbs and vitamins. These can be sourced from butchers, local shops and the internet. Many pet shops now also stock raw meats in frozen form. Advocates of BARF claim it produces benefits including:

- Smaller and less smelly stools.
- Better coat condition.
- Fewer degenerative diseases.
- Cleaner teeth.
- Increased longevity.

However, it is a controversial feeding method due to the difficulty in providing a balanced diet plus the increased risk to both dog and owner of food poisoning associated with handling and eating uncooked meat and bones. There is the added danger of bones splintering and thereby damaging teeth or causing obstructions in the gut.

Raw food diets need careful research to ensure your dog gets all the nutrients he needs.

Foods to avoid

Some foods are toxic to dogs and should never be fed:

- **Chocolate:** contains a chemical called theobromine, a toxin which can be lethal to dogs who are unable to metabolize it as rapidly or effectively as humans. Higher concentrations are found in dark than in milk chocolate, but it is safest to view all chocolate as dangerous.
- **Onions:** raw, cooked or dried cause anaemia in dogs.
- **Grapes/raisins:** just a few can cause renal failure and be fatal.

Other foods you shouldn't give your dog are cooked bones, which are brittle and can cause choking or pierce the gut wall. Also avoid adding mineral or vitamin supplements to complete foods as this can cause imbalances. Never share human food such as biscuits, cake, pizza, crisps and chips: they are too high in sugar, fats and salt.

Cat food is not suitable for dogs. The nutritional balance is wrong and it is also too high in calories. Many cat foods are also acidified, so are particularly unsuitable for puppies as this could affect skeletal growth.

Home-cooked diets

It is possible to cook meals specially for your dog, which some people feel increases the digestibility as well as the palatability of the ingredients. It is also safer than offering raw meat. Other benefits include being able to tailor the diet to the individual animal, knowing exactly what ingredients are in it, their source and quality, and being able to eliminate any that are unwanted, such as artificial preservatives, salt and other chemicals. Typical ingredients include poultry, meat, fish, eggs, vegetables and cereals or grains in the form of rice and pasta.

The downside is that it is time consuming (although with care and thought it is possible to combine cooking your own meals with those of the dog) and, even though you can store batches in the fridge or freezer, you will need to plan ahead.

WHICH FOOD IS BEST?

Whether you choose commercial or alternative foods depends on your own and your dog's personal preferences, as well as storage and the amount of time you have available.

Commercially prepared foods are not 100 per cent perfect, but they do offer convenience and, on the whole, a reasonably well-balanced diet. Organic and holistic options are available, although more expensive. When choosing between brands, price can be a good indicator: the highest-quality ingredients cost more. You tend to get what you pay for.

If you are preparing your own foods, you will need to consider what to do if you go on holiday or have to kennel your dog, when a home-made diet may not be possible. In such cases you will need to find a more convenient commercial alternative and introduce it in plenty of time beforehand.

CHANGING YOUR DOG'S FOOD

Make any changes to your dog's diet over a period of 7–10 days to avoid stomach upsets. Mix in small amounts of the new food with his usual one, gradually increasing the quantity. This applies when switching to different brands or lifestage foods as well as to new ingredients and preparation methods.

Equipment and storage

Bowls for food and water need to be big enough for the size of dog. They should either be heavy enough to stay put or have rubber bases that grip and don't move around while your dog is eating. Special designs are available to slow down greedy eaters and to keep long floppy ears out of the food. Plastic is cheap and light but may be chewed; steel is more expensive but light, durable and easy to clean; ceramic is breakable and more expensive than either plastic or steel, but harder to knock over and is hygienic.

Raised stands make eating more comfortable for long-legged breeds and older dogs.

Plastic feeding mats placed under bowls make it easy to keep floors clean and deal with spills.

Lid covers will help keep tinned foods fresh and prevent them contaminating other foodstuffs.

Store dry food in a cool, dry place.

Check manufacturers' instructions for information on correct storage and use-by dates.

Use a **measure** for dry foods to avoid overfeeding, which may happen if you judge only by eye.

Once open, store tinned food in the fridge and use within 24 hours.

Keep all foods in a place where your dog cannot access them, or fit childproof locks to the door of the cupboard where they are stored.

Keep separate **forks, spoons and washing-up utensils** for serving your dog's food and cleaning his dishes.

Drinking

Water is essential to your dog's health – it is necessary for almost every bodily function, including digestion, temperature regulation and eliminating toxic wastes. At home, your dog should have a supply of fresh water available at all times. When out on walks, carry some drinking water rather than allowing him to drink from puddles, ponds or rivers, which may be contaminated.

Avoid giving your dog milk: it can lead to diarrhoea due to an adult dog's inability to digest lactose.

Allow your dog access to fresh, clean drinking water at all times.

Signs of dehydration

Using your finger and thumb, pick up a fold of skin at the top and base of your dog's neck. The moment you release it, the skin should flatten out again. If it takes more than three seconds to do so, your dog is dehydrated and you should consult your vet. Other signs include:

- Sunken eyes.
- Loss of appetite.
- Exhaustion.
- Dry mouth (run your finger along his gums to check).
- Slow return of colour to gums when gentle pressure with a fingertip is applied and then released.

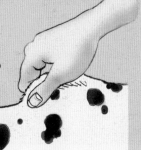

Measure dried foods carefully as it can be easy to overfeed them.

How much to feed?

If you are feeding a commercial food, follow the manufacturer's recommendations – but remember that these are only guidelines. Take into account any treats fed and, if you are using a lot during training sessions, reduce the amount of food given in meals. Obesity is a fast-growing problem in pets and can have major health repercussions, so monitor your dog's body condition and adjust the quantity accordingly. See page 111 for further information.

If giving a BARF or home-cooked diet, a general rule of thumb is to feed around 3 per cent of the dog's body weight daily, adjusting up or down according to body condition.

How often to feed?

Puppies will need feeding four times a day up to the age of three months, then three times a day until the age of six months, after which you can change to feeding twice a day. Although some owners prefer to feed just once a day, it makes it a long time between meals and may predispose your dog to bloat (see box).

If feeding twice a day, give one third of the daily intake in the morning and the rest in the evening, when your dog will be less active and have the night in which to digest it. Smaller breeds with small tummies and high metabolic rates may need feeding three times a day.

> **TIP** Your dog should be comfortable eating with you close by and he should not be encouraged to guard his food. Don't remove the bowl while he is eating unless you have to. Adding pieces of tasty food to the bowl will make your presence nearby rewarding.

> **TIP** Allow at least one hour after exercise before feeding your dog, and at least two hours after feeding before exercise.

Feeding routine

If your dog doesn't finish up his food, don't leave it out for later, but pick it up and throw it away – and don't give him anything extra at the next mealtime to compensate. This will discourage fussiness and ensure that other pets won't finish it up for him.

If you have other dogs or cats, feed them well away from each other – even in separate rooms if necessary – to prevent them stealing from each other or fighting over food. Never leave them together and unsupervised with long-lasting treats or bones for the same reason.

Allow your dog peace in which to eat his meals.

Changes in eating or drinking

Sudden changes in your dog's eating or drinking habits can indicate a health problem. Consult your vet if your dog:
- Is drinking more than usual.
- Seems constantly hungry.
- Loses or gains weight without apparent reason.
- Has not eaten for 48 hours.
- Is reluctant to eat harder foods which need more chewing.

Bloat

This is a potentially life-threatening condition in which the stomach twists, preventing gas and food from escaping. Deep-chested breeds, such as Rottweilers, are especially at risk. Other contributory factors include:
- Overfeeding.
- Stress.
- Exercising soon after a meal.
- Feeding the daily ration in one rather than splitting it into two or more meals.

Symptoms include extreme discomfort, tight and distended abdomen, retching, weakness, difficulty in breathing, rapid heart rate, salivating and lethargy.
This is a medical emergency and rapid treatment is vital – contact your vet immediately if bloat is suspected.

GROOMING

Regular grooming not only keeps your dog looking smart but also makes him feel more comfortable by removing tangles and dead hair, improving the circulation and keeping the coat and skin healthy. It also helps reinforce the bond between you.

How often?

If you have a dog with a lot of long or dense hair, you'll need to groom him thoroughly every day to prevent matts and tangles. Even with a low-maintenance coat, it's still wise to groom every day as this is an ideal opportunity to give him a quick health check (see page 109). If you have a puppy, even if his coat doesn't yet need much attention, accustom him to short grooming sessions so that it doesn't become a problem later.

Groom when your dog is relaxed, rather than full of high spirits and in the mood to play or go for a walk.

High-maintenance coats may require specialist care.

Trimming, clipping and stripping

Some dogs may require clipping and trimming to keep their coats from becoming overlong, or to reduce the amount of time needed to groom. You can either have this done at a grooming parlour, contact a freelance professional groomer who will visit your home, or learn from a groomer how to do it yourself. If you plan to show your dog, clipping must conform to set specifications (check with the breed club) and the finished result needs to look perfect, so it won't be a job for a beginner.

Certain breeds, such as the Border Terrier and Miniature Schnauzer, may need stripping rather than clipping in order to maintain the wiry texture of their coats. This involves plucking out small tufts of hair either by hand or using a special stripping knife. As with clipping, it takes practice to produce a really smart finish. Ask a groomer or breeder to show you how to do it before attempting it yourself.

Equipment

Brushes: use brushes appropriate for the coat type. Different types include:

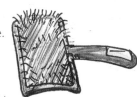

- Slicker brush to remove matted and dead hair.
- Bristle brush to remove dirt and debris – choose stiffer bristles for coarse coats, longer and more widely spaced bristles for longer coats.
- Wire-pin brush to help detangle and brush out the coat – use for woolly undercoats and curly coats.

Wide-toothed comb: use to finish off medium to long hair and thick coats. Make sure the ends are rounded so that they don't damage the skin.

Grooming glove: mitt or glove covered with rubber pimples – for dogs with short single coats, like Whippets.

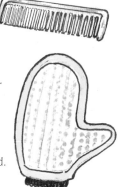

Cotton wool: to clean around eyes, nose, ears and anus.

Scissors: for any trimming needed.

Nail clippers.

Nail file: to smooth off rough edges after clipping.

Coagulant powder: to stem blood should you accidentally cut into the quick when trimming nails.

Chamois leather: for finishing the coats of short-haired single-coated dogs.

Toothbrush and toothpaste: see 'Tooth Care', page 67.

TIP If your dog dislikes being groomed, make sure you are not being too rough or using brushes too harsh for the coat. There may be a medical problem: ask your vet to check him over.

TIP Stand a small dog on a table to make grooming easier. Put a rubber mat down for a non-slip surface.

How to groom

Long, shaggy coats: start with the back legs and work your way up and forwards to the head. Concentrate on small areas at a time. Lift the top layer of hair with one hand and sweep down with the brush in the other, going with the lie of the hair and working from the roots right down to the tips. If you just brush over the surface you won't penetrate to the undercoat and it will matt up. If using a slicker brush, take care not to graze the skin.

If you come across any knots, gently tease them out with your fingers. If they are really bad, trim them out using blunt-nosed scissors and try to groom more frequently in future. Be very careful not to cut into the skin.

Use a wire-pin brush to run through the coat on the rest of the body (or a bristle brush if silky coated) and to remove any hairs that have come to the surface from the undercoat.

Gently comb through the hair around the face, ears and any feathering on the legs and tail. If your dog has long floppy ears, support each one with your free hand as you groom it.

Finish by combing gently through the coat – if you meet any resistance it means you haven't brushed it thoroughly enough.

Short-haired single-coated dogs are easier and quicker to groom: simply use a grooming glove or mitt to remove loose hairs and dry mud, and finish with a chamois leather.

If you have a dog with lots of wrinkles (such as a Bulldog), clean between the folds each day to prevent infections. Use a mild dog shampoo, rinse thoroughly and pat dry gently. Don't rub as it may chafe the skin.

Infections can occur in the deep folds of the lower lips of breeds such as St Bernards, Bloodhounds and some Spaniels. Gently washing out the pockets of skin after meals to remove saliva and food that has collected in them will help reduce the likelihood of this happening.

Finish grooming by wiping away any deposits from the corners of your dog's eyes, using a separate, moistened piece of cotton wool for each. Use another piece to clean any crusty deposits of food or mud from the nose. With one last piece, clean around the anus. If necessary, clip away any hair that tends to get soiled.

EAR CARE

Take a look inside each of your dog's ears. If they appear clean, leave them alone. A little ear wax inside the ear flaps is fine but if there is a build-up of dirt or waxy deposits, use a proprietary wax softener for canine use, then use cotton wool to swab the ear out. Alternatively you can buy special ear wipes from most pet shops. Be gentle and work from inside to outside. Never use cotton buds and avoid probing deeply into the ear – swab out only those visible and easily reached upper parts of the outer ear canal shown here.

Droopy ears, particularly if covered with hair, create ideal warm and moist conditions for organisms that cause ear infections. Carefully clipping away excess hair will allow better air circulation.

Signs that your dog may have an ear problem:

- Shaking head.
- Bad smell.
- Discharge.
- Red, inflamed ear flap.
- Tilting head.
- Sudden loss of hearing.
- Pain if the ear is touched, or reluctance to be touched.

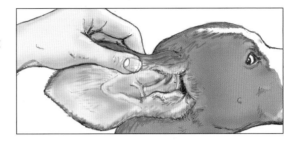

NAIL CARE

How often a dog's nails need clipping varies between individuals as well as depending on how much they move around on hard surfaces. Nails tend to grow more quickly during spring and summer. If they become overlong, they are more likely to get broken and can affect the way your dog stands and moves.

Step by step

1. Choose a time when your dog is relaxed and settled. Make sure you have good light to see by.
2. Hold the nail clippers in one hand and take your dog's paw in the other. Keep your thumb at the base of the nail you are clipping and your fingers beneath, supporting the pad.
3. Clip the nail at a 45-degree angle away from the dog, so that the tip will be parallel to the floor when the foot is put down. Clip just in front of the quick – in white nails this is easy to see as a pink line, but with black nails you will need to guess. If in doubt, just snip off the hooked tips, but do so on a frequent basis. The quick will extend further down overgrown nails, but regular trimming will encourage it to recede.
4. If you do accidentally cut into the quick, it will hurt and make your dog yelp. It may bleed quite a lot, but often looks worse than it is. Apply pressure with a clean pad for 2 minutes, or use coagulating powder to slow and stop the bleeding.
5. Finish off rough edges with a nail file so that the nails don't snag on carpeting.

If your dog dislikes nail-clipping, don't force him:

1. Accustom him to having his legs stroked and feet picked up. Reward him when he allows this.
2. Picking up a paw, pretend to clip a nail without actually doing so.
3. Try clipping just one nail on each occasion. With patience you will build up to doing more.

TOOTH CARE

By the age of three, around 70 per cent of dogs need dental treatment, so brushing your pet's teeth is important. It helps reduce the build-up of plaque, which gradually forms into tartar – a hard, brown deposit that can lead to gum disease, decay, loss of teeth and other problems.

Use a special canine toothbrush, which has a long handle, small head and very soft bristles. If you prefer, use a finger brush to introduce cleaning, but ensure it fits snugly and won't pop off in your dog's mouth. Use either clean water or a canine toothpaste; these come in a range of flavours to make them pleasant for your dog. Never use human toothpaste as this can cause gastric irritation and vomiting.

Dental chew treats, nylon chew bones and rope-type tuggy toys with a flossing action will also help keep teeth clean.

Step by step

1. Introduce cleaning when your dog is settled. Lift each jowl and gently rub a moistened finger along teeth and gums.
2. If he is happy with this, put a little toothpaste on your finger and gently rub it along teeth and gums, or use a small finger brush instead.
3. When your dog accepts this, introduce the toothbrush. Use a gentle circular motion. Concentrate on the outer surfaces where most plaque accumulates; if you can, brush the inner surfaces too. Brush at least three times a week.

Most dogs take quite happily to having their teeth brushed, but if yours really won't tolerate it, use an enzymatic oral hygiene gel (from vets or online) and apply with a finger.

Dental problems

Your dog may need to see the vet if he has:

- Bad breath.
- Drooling.
- Dislike of crunchy foods.
- Nasal discharge.
- Facial swellings.
- Red/bleeding gums.
- Tartar formation.
- Loss of/loose teeth.

Clean regularly to avoid problems.

Bathing your dog

The occasional bath will help make your dog more socially acceptable, as well as more pleasant to have around your home. Don't bathe him too frequently as it will strip his coat and skin of their natural oils, leaving them dry. Unless he has rolled in something smelly, once every two or three months will generally be sufficient.

WHAT YOU WILL NEED

Get everything ready before you start. Use a bath or a shower tray, or even the kitchen sink if you have a very small dog.

A shower attachment to make wetting and rinsing the coat easy.

A non-slip rubber mat to protect surfaces from being scratched and to give your dog a secure footing.

A sponge to help wash the face.

A shampoo specifically designed for dogs, as these are usually low-lather, making them easier to rinse out and suitably mild so they don't irritate the skin. Read the manufacturer's instructions before applying, as some shampoos may need to be diluted before use.

A plastic measuring jug for rinsing.

Several large bath towels for drying.

PREPARING YOUR DOG

Before you start, groom your dog thoroughly, as loose hairs will clog up plugholes and shampoo won't penetrate matted fur very well. Any tangles will also knot themselves up even more tightly once they're wet.

- If your dog normally wears a leather collar, replace it with a nylon or cotton-web one which will neither be damaged if it gets wet nor leach coloured dyes which will stain your dog's coat. If he is wearing an insecticidal collar, remove this too.
- If you are using a shower tray, simply encourage your dog to step in. If you are using a bath or sink, lift him in rather than trying to persuade him to jump in, which could result in an injury.
- Remember, you may need help. Some dogs hate having baths, even though they may let no opportunity pass to jump into ponds, rivers and puddles when out on walks.

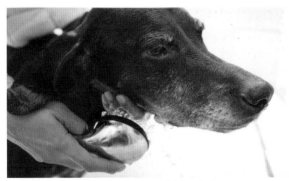

A flexible shower attachment is useful for rinsing.

Professional help

If you do not have the facilities, or need assistance but don't have anyone to help you, try contacting a mobile dog-washing service, who will come to you with their own self-contained unit and all the necessary equipment.

Alternatively, you could take your dog along to a dog-grooming parlour. Look in your local telephone or Yellow Pages directory; your vet or a dog-training club may also be able to recommend one to you.

WASHING

Always begin with your dog's body, including legs and tail, and leave the head until last.

- Check the water temperature – use lukewarm water.
- Wet the coat well, working from top to bottom and front to back, talking to your dog as you do so to reassure him.
- Once the coat is completely saturated, massage shampoo into it well, working in the same order as when wetting.

Washing the head

Leave the head till last.

- Point the head upwards to avoid suds in your dog's eyes, ears or mouth.
- Using a sponge will give you better control over the water flow, and may be less frightening for your dog.
- It's usually at this point, when the head and neck are wet as well as the body, that your dog is likely to shake himself. Be ready for it!

RINSING

Rinse off the shampoo thoroughly, starting at the head and working from top to bottom and front to rear as before.

Keep rinsing until the water runs completely clear and there are no signs of any suds when you rub hairs between your fingers. Any soap left behind will make his coat look dull and may cause itchiness.

DRYING

Squeeze any excess water from your dog's coat with your hands, then use a towel to dry off the worst of the wet before you lift him from the bath.

If the coat is very thick, even though the top layers of hair seem dry, he may still be damp underneath. Try using a hairdryer to finish off. Use the lowest heat, don't hold it too close, and keep it moving, parting thick or long coats with your fingers.

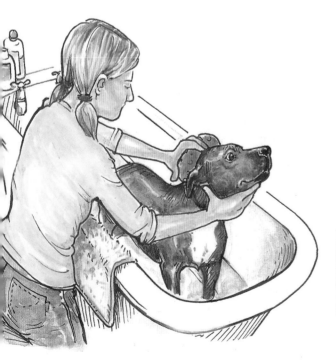

EXERCISE

Adequate exercise is essential for your dog's emotional as well as his physical well-being. Even small dogs with low exercise requirements will enjoy and benefit from daily walks.

What's right for your dog?

Different breeds have different requirements in terms of duration and type of exercise; some will need plenty of space and opportunity for free running as well as leash walks, while others will be happy taking a gentle stroll and enjoying a romp in the park. You may need to take particular care not to over-exercise some breeds while they are still growing as this can lead to joint damage.

Strong hunting instincts and/or poor recall (see page 91) may mean that it isn't safe to allow some dogs off the leash, so you may need to find a securely enclosed area where yours can let off steam if he is an active breed who needs to be able to run.

Some dogs enjoy going out jogging with their owners, and this particular activity has given rise to the increasingly popular cani-cross competitions – see page 101 for more information. You can take your dog running with you provided he is of a breed that can cope with this type of extended-duration exertion, but it shouldn't be a substitute for slower-paced walks, both on and off the leash.

Going out with your dog isn't just about taking exercise – it is also an opportunity for mental stimulation, allowing him to explore, meet people and other dogs, and for the two of you to interact with each other.

Activities to avoid

Cycling with your dog is not a good idea. You may go too fast, too far and for too long without being aware of the fact that your dog is struggling. Neither do you have proper control over his actions, which could be dangerous for both of you as well as for others.

The same applies to your dog accompanying you while you are on horseback: if anything were to happen to your dog, you would not be able to attend to him properly while also keeping good control of the horse.

> **TIP** Avoid taking your dog out during the hottest parts of the day in summer – walk him during the early morning and in the evening when it is cooler. See page 115 for information on heatstroke.

All dogs need daily exercise, although how much varies depending on age, breed, fitness and any health issues.

Going for a walk

Ideally, walking your dog should include time interacting with each other as well as allowing him free running. Take along a favourite toy and stop occasionally to play a game such as hide and seek. Introduce short training sessions. When walking on the leash you can also take varying routes, stop and start, ask him to sit and wait, zigzag, change direction and change your speed to make things a little unpredictable and encourage him to keep his eye on you. These tactics will help keep walks interesting, reinforce habits of obedience in different situations and strengthen the bond between you.

WALKING SAFETY

When you are walking your dog, be sure to take all the personal safety precautions that are advised for anyone walking in either a town or the countryside. It is important to remember that the presence of your dog in no way guarantees your safety and you should do all you can to keep yourself and your pet free from harm. In addition:

- Don't allow your dog to disturb animals or wildlife; keep him on the leash at all times when near livestock. Especially when they have young, livestock and deer may behave aggressively if they consider you or your dog to be a threat.
- Your dog must wear a collar and ID with your name and address on it – this is a legal requirement and will also increase the likelihood that you will be reunited should he become lost (see page 72).
- If using a retractable lead, keep it shortened and with the brake on when walking along roads and pavements.
- If your dog enters a river or runs out on to a frozen pond, *never* follow him, even if he seems to be in difficulty. Every year tragedies occur when people lose their footing or fall through ice as they try to rescue their pet.

SCOOP UP POOP

Always scoop your dog's poop. Use a bag to pick it up, then seal it and place it in a dog-waste bin. If there isn't one nearby, either take it home to dispose of it or put it in an ordinary litter bin, having double-bagged it first.

Taking your dog for a walk offers opportunities for interaction as well as exercise.

After your walk

On returning from a walk, you should always check your dog over for:

- Grass seeds that have become trapped between his toes.
- Ticks, which are easily picked up in long grass and undergrowth (see page 112).
- Damaged or broken toenails.
- Cuts or grazes on his pads and anywhere else on his body.
- Toxic substances – in winter, rinse paws in warm water to remove any salt that has been put down on pavements, or traces of coolant spilled from car radiators.

What to take with you

For your own and your dog's safety, keep the following things in a bag ready to take with you when you go for a walk:

- Dog treats
- Mobile phone
- Personal alarm
- Pocket first aid kit
- Poop bags
- Water
- Whistle

LOST DOG

Losing your dog can be very distressing. As well as the danger of your dog straying too far and getting lost, theft is also on the increase, with pets being stolen and ransomed or used as breeding stock on puppy farms and for other illegal activities.

Preventing loss or theft

The following precautions can reduce the risk of your dog being lost or stolen:

- Neutering will reduce the likelihood of a male dog straying in search of a bitch on heat (see page 111).
- Teach good recall and 'Leave it' commands (see pages 91 and 88), practising them every day to reinforce them so you stand a better chance of getting your dog to come back, even in highly distracting situations.
- Don't let your dog off the leash if you don't have a good recall, or in areas where you know he won't be able to resist chasing after rabbits or squirrels.
- Establish a good door routine so that your dog doesn't dash past you when you open it (see page 105).
- Make sure your garden is securely fenced and check boundaries every day (see pages 50–51).
- Don't take your dog out when fireworks are being let off, or if it is thundery, in case he becomes scared by the noise and runs off.
- Always keep an eye on your dog while out in the garden, and never leave him tied up outside a shop or in an unlocked car, as these are places where thieves may strike.
- Fit an alarm or bell to garden gates to alert you to the presence of intruders.

Don't leave your dog tied up in places where he is at risk of being stolen.

MICROCHIPPING

Having your dog microchipped will ensure that, should he lose his collar with its ID tag (see page 73), he can still be identified and safely returned to you. A microchip containing all your details is inserted just beneath the skin – it is about the size of a small grain of rice and the procedure takes just seconds. Once in position it causes no discomfort and it provides permanent identification. The information can be read using a special hand-held scanner.

Ask your vet to check the microchip whenever you take your dog for a health check to see that it is still functioning and in position. If you change address, make sure you inform the register so that your details can be updated.

If your dog is lost or stolen

- Contact police, dog warden, local rescue centres and vets in your area (your dog may need treatment if found injured). Contact them all each day your dog is missing; sometimes information isn't shared or is slow to percolate through.
- If he is microchipped, you should quickly inform the appropriate register.
- Check the area around the place where your dog went missing. Ask anyone prepared to help to search, giving them a supply of your dog's favourite treats.
- Print off posters, preferably with a good recent photograph of your dog, including details of any distinguishing characteristics, your contact details and stating whether a reward is offered. Ask if your posters can be displayed at kennels, veterinary practices, pet shops and feed merchants, pubs, social clubs, libraries, village halls, training clubs and anywhere else you can think of.
- Post details on canine-interest websites, in particular those specifically concerned with lost and stolen pets.
- Contact your insurance company, as you may be able to claim for advertising and reward costs.
- Place advertisements in local newspapers and ask for publicity from local radio stations.

TIP When reporting the loss or theft of your dog, give as precise a description as possible. Not everyone is an expert on breeds so providing a photo helps.

TIP Have someone stay at home by the phone while you are out searching in case there is news of your dog.

If you find a stray

If you find a stray dog, you are legally required either to return him to his owner if known, or to contact your local council, who will arrange for him to be collected by the dog warden. The authorities will keep the dog for a minimum of seven days, after which they may either rehome him or have him put to sleep. If you want to look after him yourself, the authorities will first need to check that you are a suitable person and you will be legally obliged to keep the dog for one month to give the original owners time to claim him.

LEGAL RESPONSIBILITIES

An important, if often overlooked, part of caring for your dog is being aware of your legal responsibilities as an owner. Many countries have legislation regarding dogs, including which breeds you can own, where you can take them and what you can do with them.

OWNERSHIP

Many countries ban certain breeds and breed crosses, and require others to be on a lead at all times in public, and possibly also to be muzzled. In some places insurance cover must be held. Some cities and districts also impose restrictions on the number of dogs you are allowed to own or to walk at the same time.

As you are generally held to be liable for your dog's actions, it is sensible to take out third party public liability insurance, even if it is not compulsory.

DANGEROUS DOGS

In the UK it is a criminal offence under the Dangerous Dogs Act to allow a dog to be 'dangerously out of control' in a public place. This doesn't just mean a dog that has injured someone, but any dog that causes someone to have 'reasonable apprehension' that it may do so. A dog chasing, barking at, or jumping up at a person, even though it may be in fun, could lead to a complaint, so it is important to keep your dog under good control and ensure that he is well trained. Should he be the subject of a complaint, he could be seized and possibly destroyed, while you could be prosecuted, fined or even jailed. A number of other European countries and the USA also have 'dangerous dog' legislation.

CLEANING UP AFTER YOUR DOG

Make sure you don't fall foul of the law by failing to pick up after your pet. In the UK it can result in a fine of up to £1,000. Leaving your dog's faeces is not only unsociable and unhygienic, but will do little to endear dogs to the rest of your neighbourhood and could actively contribute to the ever-increasing amounts of anti-dog legislation.

LEASH LAWS

In the UK it is an offence to walk your dog off the leash on a designated road. In the US, dogs are generally required to be kept on a leash and under control whenever they are off their owner's property, except in a specially designated dog park where they can run free.

Finding out your responsibilities

Laws can vary considerably between countries, or even between states or regions within a country. The Kennel Club of the country you live in should be able to advise on any legislation that may affect you. If you plan to take your dog abroad, check with DEFRA (in the UK) and the embassy or tourist board of the country you'll be visiting.

BARKING

Frequent prolonged barking can be a real nuisance to neighbours, although usually the owner of the dog is unaware of the problem as it happens while they are out. If the local council receives a complaint, an environmental officer will investigate and may suggest a course of action. If the dog owner does not comply, an abatement notice may be served, possibly followed by prosecution and a fine of up to £5,000.

PLACES DOGS CAN'T GO

Many cities have restrictions on where you can exercise dogs, both on and off the leash. Some areas of beaches may be subject to either year-round or seasonal bans.

Keep your dog on a short leash near farm animals. In the UK, if he chases or worries livestock, the farmer has a legal right to shoot him.

ID

In the UK, any dog in a public place must wear a collar with the name and address, including postcode, of the owner written or engraved on it or on an attached tag. A telephone number is optional but advisable, as it will make it easier for you to be contacted in the event of your dog getting lost and being found by someone.

VACCINATION

Rabies is not present in the UK, but vaccination against it is compulsory if you want to take your pet abroad under the Pet Passport Scheme (see page 95). In much of the US and Europe rabies vaccination is compulsory.

LICENCE

Although a dog licence is not required in the UK, it is mandatory in most states of the US and in some European countries. Fees are sometimes higher if the dog isn't neutered, and it may be necessary to produce proof of rabies vaccination before a licence can be purchased.

OTHER LAWS

There are many other laws relevant to dogs and owners, including legislation on straying, docking (the brutal removal of most of a dog's tail), dog-fighting, breeding, welfare, chaining and even travelling with a dog in your car. Contact your country's Kennel Club for advice.

Chapter 4

TEACHING YOUR DOG

When you get a new puppy or dog, he'll need to learn how to behave with people, dogs and other animals, and in different environments and situations. He'll also have to learn to perform specific actions when you ask him, such as sitting, lying down or coming to you when you call. Both types of training are important to help him develop into a well-balanced and confident individual who fits in happily with you and your family and is fun to have around.

Training isn't just for newly acquired puppies and dogs, but is an ongoing process that should continue throughout your pet's lifetime. Revising what he has already learned will keep him up to scratch, while teaching new things will provide mental stimulation. The interaction involved in training, as well as the need to communicate clearly, is also an important part of your relationship with your dog.

SOCIALIZATION

Puppies develop very quickly in comparison to humans, so they need to get accustomed to an enormous number of stimuli in a very short time if they are to become confident adults. Dogs who have not been adequately socialized from an early age are more likely to develop phobias and fears, and may find it difficult to cope with anything new or unusual.

What is socialization?

Socialization means getting your puppy used to a wide range of sights, sounds, smells, places, people and animals, and teaching him to be confident and relaxed about them.

Puppies have a 'sensitive' period lasting until they are 12–16 weeks old. During this time they will tolerate, enjoy and be curious about everything new they encounter, but after it they may view new experiences with caution and even fear. Therefore the more things with which you can familiarize your puppy early in his life, the better. It is also important to build on this aspect of his education throughout his life in order to maintain confidence.

START EARLY

Your puppy's breeder plays an important part in getting him off to a good start and should have spent time handling him, introducing outings in the car, accustoming him to life indoors and to the comings and goings of visitors.

Do not assume this has been the case, though – ask what has been done.

When you take your puppy home, you will need to be careful about where you take him until his primary course of vaccinations is complete (see page 111). However, it is important to go out and about with him, even if you have to carry him to prevent him from coming into contact with areas where unvaccinated dogs may have passed.

TIP If you see another dog being walked on a leash in an area where free running is permitted, there is probably a very good reason for it. Put yours on the leash too until you are well past.

Meeting other dogs

For the safety of all concerned, encounters with other dogs should be carefully managed rather than just allowed to happen. Never allow your dog to run straight up to another – although your dog may be friendly, the other may be scared or aggressive.

Teach your dog good 'meet and greet' manners with the help of another dog who is steady, obedient and well socialized. If you do not have a friend with a dog who fits the bill, ask a trainer for help.

1. Ask your dog to sit and keep his attention focused on you as the other dog walks past at a distance (see pages 84–85). Use high-value treats (see page 79) and be generous with them, as it is difficult for some dogs to contain their excitement when they spot a potential friend nearby. Gradually decrease the distance at which the other dog walks past you.
2. Reverse the situation: while the other dog sits, walk yours past, rewarding him for keeping his attention on you.
3. Vary things a little further by having the dogs walk together, first of all moving in the same direction and then going in opposite directions. When your dog can manage this with ease, make it a little more demanding by having the other dog jog past in both directions.

This exercise may take a little time to teach, but it is worth the effort. Teaching your dog to look at you when another approaches rather than making direct eye contact with it can help defuse any tension. It also reinforces your authority and encourages him to ask you for permission before interacting with another dog.

Teaching good manners when meeting other dogs is worth the effort and can help avoid unpleasant encounters.

New experiences are important – but too much at once can overwhelm a puppy, making him feel anxious rather than confident.

Make new experiences enjoyable

Everything your puppy learns while young will have a lasting impact for better or worse, so when exposing him to new experiences you need to try to ensure he develops positive associations with them. This means you will need to plan carefully and engineer encounters so that he is not stressed or scared by them.

- Take him first to quiet locations and slowly build up to more complex situations, such as a busy town street or playground.
- Don't force him to approach things he finds alarming.
- Increase the number of new experiences gradually – young puppies tire quickly and are easily overwhelmed.

MAKE A LIST OF NEW EXPERIENCES

List as many things as you can think of to which you can introduce your puppy and tick them off as you meet them. Your list might include:

Dealing with anxiety

Signs that your puppy may feel anxious:
- Trembling.
- Trying to hide.
- Growling.
- Urinating.
- Snapping.

Don't make an issue of it: over-reassuring him can make it appear that you are concerned yourself and that there really is something to be scared of. Slowly move away from whatever is causing the anxiety, be patient and give him the time he needs to get used to it. Reward him with high-value treats (see page 79) each time he doesn't react. As he becomes bolder, gradually move closer.

People
- ☐ Tall and short, young and old.
- ☐ Beards and moustaches.
- ☐ Different ethnic backgrounds.
- ☐ Different clothes and hats.
- ☐ Carrying items, including bags, walking sticks and umbrellas.
- ☐ In wheelchairs, mobility scooters, with walking frames.
- ☐ Postman, dustman.

At home
- ☐ Vacuum cleaner.
- ☐ Washing machine.
- ☐ Dishwasher.
- ☐ Telephone.
- ☐ Television.
- ☐ Doorbell/doorknocker.
- ☐ Music system.

Outdoors
- ☐ Lawnmowers.
- ☐ Buses, cars, lorries, motorcycles.
- ☐ Trains.
- ☐ Aeroplanes.
- ☐ Joggers.
- ☐ Cyclists.
- ☐ Different surfaces, including gravel, grass, sand, tarmac.

Places
- ☐ Fêtes and car-boot sales.
- ☐ Playgrounds.
- ☐ Shops.
- ☐ Towns.
- ☐ Fairgrounds.

Animals
- ☐ Other dogs.
- ☐ Cats.
- ☐ Birds.
- ☐ Horses.
- ☐ Sheep.
- ☐ Cows.
- ☐ Goats.
- ☐ Rabbits.

HOME ALONE

As well as learning how to behave in company, your dog also needs to learn how to cope when left on his own. The closer the bond you have with him, the more important it is to teach this to prevent him becoming distressed when you aren't around.

Teaching your dog to be on his own

It's easier for both of you if you begin to teach your dog to deal with being on his own sooner rather than later. While you may find it flattering that he wants to be with you all the time, if you can't go to another room without his insisting on accompanying you, he may become highly agitated when you do have to leave him home alone.

Don't allow him constant free access to you when you are in the house – but introduce separation gradually, or you may create the anxiety you are trying to avoid.

1. Wait until your dog is playing with a toy or chewing a long-lasting treat, then quietly leave the room, shutting the door behind you.
2. Wait a second or two, open the door and re-enter the room. Quietly greet him, but don't make a big fuss of him as this will excite him and emphasize the fact that you have been absent.
3. Repeat as frequently as possible during the day, slowly extending the length of time you are on the other side of the door. If he barks or scratches at the door, wait until he is quiet before going back in so that he doesn't associate his actions with your return.
4. As he becomes more relaxed about being left, start getting him used to you leaving through the front door. Once again, start with periods of just a few seconds and gradually increase the duration.

MAKE BEING AT HOME A PLEASANT EXPERIENCE

The most stressful time for your dog is the period immediately after you leave. Help him cope by:
- Making a calm exit without fussing over him.
- Leaving a blanket that smells of you in his bed.
- Giving him a Kong (see page 93) tightly packed with tasty treats. This helps create a pleasant association with your departure and gives him something to occupy his mind. Chewing at it to extract the food will also release calming endorphins into his system. To keep this treat special, pick up the Kong when you return.
- Leave a radio on at low volume, tuned in to a chat show or classical music station.
- A DAP diffuser may be helpful with some dogs (see page 45).

Before you go out you should also:
- Make sure he has relieved himself.
- Ensure he has had sufficient exercise, while avoiding games that will over-excite him.

Dogs that can't cope

A dog who is distressed at being left on his own can become noisy, destructive and may soil around the house. See page 106 for more information on separation anxiety.

Begin to introduce short periods alone gradually and make them as pleasant an experience as possible.

CAR TRAVEL

Spend time introducing your dog to the car and teaching him to travel quietly and confidently, otherwise even short trips can become an ordeal for both of you and may limit the places you can take him.

Even though you may take great care in introducing car travel, not all dogs are good passengers. See page 107 for more information on helping dogs who suffer from motion sickness and other travelling problems.

Introducing the car

Familiarize your dog with being in the car and build up positive associations with it in easy stages. If you have a puppy, the earlier you begin, the better.

1. Start by letting your dog become accustomed to being in the car while it is stationary. If necessary, use a treat to encourage him into the area in which he will be travelling. Praise and reward him, but avoid making such a big fuss of him that he becomes over-excited.

2. Let him out again, then repeat this several times, gradually extending the length of time he is in the car. You can even feed some of his meals in the car to help make it a pleasurable experience.

3. When he seems relaxed about it, start the engine and allow it to run while the car remains stationary.

4. When he is unconcerned about this, try going for a short drive. A few minutes will be fine the first time or two, then gradually increase the duration of each trip.

If introduced carefully, most dogs will enjoy going for a car ride.

Travelling safely

For his own safety as well as that of you and any passengers, your dog should be contained in some way when travelling in the car.

Dog guard. This will help confine your dog to the rear or boot area. It is cheap to buy and easy to install, allows plenty of room and will prevent him interfering with the driver. Guards can be dislodged by the dog, however, and will not prevent him being thrown around, possibly injuring himself and others in an accident.

Seat belt. A padded harness which attaches to the car's own seatbelt system. Take time to introduce it in easy steps. Unsuitable for puppies, and some dogs may dislike the restriction.

Pet carrier or crate. This is the safest way to travel with your dog, but make sure that it is secured to prevent it sliding around. Small carriers can be placed on a rear seat and the seatbelt restraint placed over them. Wire crates allow for better ventilation than plastic carriers and can be folded flat for storage. Permanent car kennelling systems which fit to the contours of the car can be bought. Soft carriers are not suitable, as bored or stressed dogs can easily chew or claw their way out. Most dogs are happy to travel in a carrier or crate if it has been introduced properly (see page 60).

Other safety considerations

- Never allow your dog to travel with his head out of the window – ear, eye or nose injuries could result.
- If your dog travels on a rear seat and you are parked on a road, get him in and out from the kerb side, away from passing traffic.
- Put your dog's leash on before taking him out of the car and teach him to wait for you to tell him he can get out.
- Never position your dog in the car next to an airbag.
- **Never leave your dog alone in the car in summer.** Even in mild weather with the windows open there is a danger of him overheating.

BASIC OBEDIENCE

Teaching your dog basic obedience is important for his safety as well as that of others. Once established, it ensures you are able to control him in a variety of situations. It also helps make him easier and more enjoyable to have around, and forms the foundation for all other activities you may want to try with him (see Chapter 5).

Equipment and tools

Collar: pick one of suitable size, type and strength for your dog and which fits so that you can comfortably insert two fingers between collar and neck. A martingale-type collar may be a good choice for a narrow-skulled dog, such as a Greyhound or Lurcher, to prevent it from sliding off over his head, but otherwise a plain flat collar is best. Avoid choke, prong or shock collars, which can be both damaging and frightening.

Harness: this can make it easier to contain a dog who bounces around a lot when learning to walk on the leash. Choose one of the non-tightening sort that you can adjust to a good fit. Check regularly for any signs of chafing behind the front legs and around the chest. Your dog will still need to wear a collar with ID when out in public (see page 73).

Toys: can be used both to help motivate your dog and to reward him. Grade them just as you would food.

Treat pouch: a pouch or bag is useful for keeping treats to hand, especially greasier kinds which soil pockets. Leave small pots of treats around the house (out of reach of your dog) so that you can train him anywhere at any time.

Food treats: for luring your dog into performing a desired action (see page 80), as well as to reward him when he achieves it. Keep a variety available, graded according to desirability. The highest-value, 'five-star' treats will be the tastiest (e.g. cheese, morsels of frankfurter or cooked chicken); reserve these for an extra good effort or when introducing something new. The lowest value, 'one star' treats will be less exciting, such as a piece of plain biscuit.

Long line leash – anything from 10–20 metres long and made of light cotton or nylon web. Helpful when teaching recall (see page 91) and retrieve exercises if you think your dog might try to run off. Clip on to a harness rather than the collar to avoid neck injury. Wear gloves to prevent friction burns.

Short leash – use when walking your dog close by your side. Choose one that is comfortable to hold, appropriate to your dog's size and strength and long enough to reach from your hand to his collar with some slack.

Teaching your dog to take a treat gently

If your dog tends to grab at food treats when you offer them, teach him to take them more gently in the following way:

1. Take a small piece of food and grip it firmly between thumb and forefinger.
2. Offer it to him: if he tries to snatch it, keep your hand in the same position, but don't let go of the treat. Release it only when he slows down and takes it gently.
3. Start off using one-star treats (see above) and build up to offering more desirable ones.

Teaching techniques

Teach your dog in a way that is fun and enjoyable for both of you – punishment or physical force tends to be ineffective, confrontational, creates fear and destroys trust between you. Dogs tend to repeat behaviours they find rewarding but not those that aren't, so reward-based training works very effectively with most.

LURE AND REWARD

The easiest way to train your dog to perform an action is to lure him into producing the action that you want with a treat. This works on the principle that where his nose goes, his body will follow. See pages 84–91 for how to train your dog to watch you and to sit, lie down, stand, stay, leave, give, walk on the leash, and return to you.

When to reward your dog

- Reward your dog as soon as he performs the action you want, otherwise he won't associate the two.
- Once he understands what you want him to do, vary the type and value of reward so he doesn't know what he's going to get. If it's too predictable he may begin to ignore it. Keep him guessing.
- Don't take good behaviour for granted – notice, praise and reward it once it's been learned, not just while teaching it.
- Reward only those actions you want; ignore those you don't.

HOW TO REWARD

Rewards for your dog include praise, petting, food and play. The last two will be the most desirable to him.

Most dogs are motivated by food: if yours isn't interested in what you are offering, maybe you haven't yet found anything tempting enough. For the greatest success, your dog needs to be hungry enough really to want food treats, but not so desperate that all he can do is concentrate on the food instead of on what he needs to do to earn it.

Use an appropriate level of treat for the task you are asking your dog to perform, using a high-level reward for new actions or those he finds particularly hard and reducing the level of reward once it is well established. Using the highest-value treat too often will devalue it and your dog may refuse to work for anything less. It will also leave you with nothing better to tempt him with in a really challenging situation.

If you are using a lot of food treats, reduce his daily food ration to prevent him gaining weight. Divide treats into tiny pieces so they are easy to eat quickly and don't fill your dog up too fast.

Another form of reward is to release your dog to an activity he finds enjoyable. For example, having asked him to come back to you, reward him by sending him off again to play.

Use toys as rewards if your dog is more motivated by them than by food – but having to stop to play can be time consuming and it may not always be safe or convenient. Ideally, try to get your dog more interested in food than in toys, and keep toys as an exciting alternative.

Food can be used to encourage your dog to perform different actions: this is known as 'lure and reward'.

Hand Signals and Body Language

Once you have taught your dog an action, you can add a hand signal just before asking for the action: he will quickly begin to connect the two and respond to the signal. It is easiest if the hand signal is similar to the movement you made when luring him – for example, raising your hand to ask him to sit or gesturing downwards to ask him to lie down.

Take care that your body language can't be interpreted as threatening: don't loom over your dog and avoid staring hard at him. You can also use body language to encourage a better response: moving backwards as you call him can speed up a slow recall (see page 91), while turning your body sideways may be less intimidating if he tends to be nervous.

Voice

Your voice can be used to:
- Praise your dog when he's done something right.
- Give verbal cues for actions.
- Interrupt unwanted behaviours.

When praising, raise the pitch of your voice and really try to get your pleasure across.

If you need to stop him doing something you don't want, a sharp 'ah-ah' should be sufficient. Having got his attention, give him an alternative action to perform.

Generally, only attach a verbal cue to an action once he can produce it fairly consistently in response to your hand signal. Decide what words you will use for each action and then stick to them. A change in cue word will confuse him. You should also:

- Speak clearly.
- Never shout.
- Say a cue word only once: don't keep repeating it, or he will learn to ignore it.
- Avoid using lots of words together as he won't be able to pick out the cue word from a whole sentence.
- Prefix a cue word with your dog's name first to gain his attention.
- Give an appropriate cue word for the action you want and don't use the same cue word for different actions. If your dog understands 'Down' means lie down, you can't expect him to understand it also means 'Get off the sofa'.

Release word

Teaching a 'release' word tells your dog when an exercise has finished – if he doesn't know, he may decide to 'release' himself before you're ready. Having a release word will also make it easier when teaching stays of longer duration, or a more complex series of actions. Use a word such as 'OK!' in an excited tone and encourage him to move around or play with a toy.

Reward your dog by praising or petting him, offering a food treat or playing a brief but exciting game with a favourite toy.

Clicker training

You may like to try teaching your dog by using a clicker. This can be a very effective method and can be used with all dogs, young and old. A clicker is a small plastic box with a metal

tongue inside which makes a distinctive 'click' when pressed with your thumb. Your dog learns to associate the sound with a reward and, once the connection has been made, every time he hears it he'll know that:

- What he was doing at that precise moment was good.
- A reward will follow shortly.
- The exercise is finished.

An alternative to the clicker is to use a word such as 'Good!' or 'Yes!' as a marker. Teach the association with a reward in the same way as with a clicker, but beware of using the word accidentally on other occasions or you may teach an action you didn't intend!

LEARNING TO USE A CLICKER ACCURATELY

Practise operating the clicker out of earshot of your dog before using it with him so that you learn to be accurate and observant. This is important, as the noise should mark the precise moment that your dog produces the action you want him to repeat. If you are slow off the mark, you may end up teaching him something completely different. You can practise by:

- Tossing a ball in the air and clicking at the exact moment it hits the ground, or as it reaches the top of its arc.
- Throwing a ball against a wall and clicking as it touches it.
- Watching someone walking and clicking each time their left (or right) foot touches the ground.

When using a clicker

- Click only once each time.
- It's not a remote control – don't point it at him or hold it near his ears.
- Don't use it to try to gain his attention.

INTRODUCING THE CLICKER TO YOUR DOG

Teach your dog to associate the sound of the clicker with a food treat.

1 **Place a bowl of tasty treats within easy reach. Don't have them in your pocket or hand, as your dog needs to learn to concentrate on you and the sound of the clicker, not on the food.**

2 **Sound the clicker, holding it behind your back as you do so.**

3 **Immediately give your dog a treat. As he begins to anticipate** the treat, start to vary the length of time between the click and giving the food by 1–5 seconds. He will soon understand that, even though the treat doesn't arrive instantly, it will definitely follow once he's heard the clicker.

4 **Repeat 20–30 times. Some dogs learn very quickly, others may need several sessions. As soon** as he has made the association you can begin using the clicker as a training aid. Do this either by waiting for a behaviour to happen, then click and treat, or by using food or a toy to lure him into the position you want him to be in, then giving a click and treat.

5 **A clicker is a teaching tool, so you don't need to use it for ever, only when teaching new actions.** Once your dog has learned to respond to a hand signal and verbal cue, you no longer need to use the clicker when asking for that action.

Training classes should be fun as well as instructive for both you and your dog.

Taking your dog to classes

As well as teaching your dog at home, enrolling him in a class can help him learn to interact politely with other dogs and to stay focused on you in their presence. Classes also offer you encouragement and help if you have a problem.

TYPES OF CLASS

Puppy classes. These enable your puppy to meet others and to begin learning some training basics. The wrong class can do more harm than good, so check it out before enrolling. In a good class you will find:
- Play sessions restricted to two or three carefully selected pups at a time, to avoid bullying and over-rough interaction. A class should not be a chaotic free-for-all.
- An age limit of around 20 weeks, so all puppies are at a similar stage of development.
- At least one trainer for every eight puppies.

Courses. These offer further training after puppy classes. Running for a specified number of weeks, they have a set number of people per class, handouts are often included, and they can offer you and your dog a good grounding or help you progress to the next level of training.

Clubs. Training clubs usually run classes each week, but the number of people attending can vary each time. Some specialize in activities such as agility or flyball (see pages 100 and 101), while others offer general obedience and fun training. Most encourage you to continue teaching your dog beyond the basics and many have a social element.

One-to-one training. If your dog is reactive with others, finds it too stressful to cope with a class, or if you want to teach him a specialist skill, then one-to-one tuition tailored to your needs may be more appropriate.

VISIT CLASSES BEFORE YOU TAKE YOUR DOG

Always check out a class without your dog before enrolling; you may find it helpful to visit several and compare them. A good class should have a friendly atmosphere and you should feel comfortable with the training methods, which should be fun and reward-based. Other points to look for include:
- Patient, knowledgeable, enthusiastic and articulate trainers.
- No shouting and not too much barking.
- One trainer for every 6–8 dogs.
- No use of choke chains, smacking or physical force.
- A secure spacious venue with a suitable surface: slippery floors can be dangerous and may make some dogs anxious.

Finding a training class

Details of local classes can be found in:
- Veterinary practices and rescue shelters.
- Yellow Pages and the local press.
- Noticeboards at pet shops.

You can also ask dog-owning friends for recommendations, or contact the Association of Pet Dog Trainers (APDT UK) to find trainers in your area (see page 126). All APDT members are insured and are committed to using only fair and humane training methods.

BASIC OBEDIENCE EXERCISES

If your dog struggles to learn any of the following exercises, it may be because you are trying to progress too fast, so go back to the last successful step, take things more slowly and make sure rewards are sufficiently motivating. A physical problem could also be responsible for difficulties – if you aren't sure, give your dog the benefit of the doubt and ask your vet to check him over.

Teaching your dog his name

Say your dog's name in a bright, happy voice. If he looks at you, praise him and give him a treat.

Always repeat his name just before you put his lead on, make a fuss of him, give him his tea, invite him to have a game or do anything else that he views as enjoyable. He will soon learn to look at you when he hears his name in expectation of something happening. You can then use this during teaching to get his attention before asking him to do something.

Teaching 'Watch Me'

This helps increase your dog's ability to concentrate, as well as ensuring that you can gain – and keep – his undivided attention when you need it.

TIP Experiment with the position in which you hold the treat when first teaching this – under your chin, beside your eye, on top of your head or even just behind it. Use the position that best encourages your dog to make eye contact.

1 Show your dog that you have a tasty treat, then slowly bring it up towards your face. His eyes will follow the food as it moves upwards.

2 Wait to give him the treat until he shifts his gaze from the food to make eye contact with you. This may be only a momentary flicker of a glance to start with, so be ready to praise and reward as soon as it happens.

3 When he can manage a couple of seconds' eye contact, attach first a hand signal and then a verbal cue such as 'Watch', 'Watch me' or 'Look'. Gradually build up the amount of time you can maintain the eye contact.

Keeping up training

Among other benefits, teaching your dog new things throughout his life helps to keep his brain active, and it is thought that it can help to reduce the effects of Canine Cognitive Dysfunction (see page 123).

Training tips

- Keep training sessions short and fun – puppies and some adult dogs have short attention spans and tire quickly. Several short sessions are more effective than one long one. Aim for a 3-minute session with a puppy.
- Train in lots of different places so that your dog learns to obey you regardless of where he is. You may find it necessary to use higher-value treats when you are away from home with lots of distractions.
- Make sure the surface you are training on isn't slippery. If his paws slide around, it will make the exercise harder and may make him anxious.
- Finish on a good note – a well-rewarded success will make your dog, and you, look forward to the next training session.

Teaching 'Sit'

Teaching your dog to sit when greeting people can make him seem less frightening to those who are nervous of dogs. It also teaches him polite greeting behaviour, pre-empting any inclination to jump up.

TIP Find lots of different occasions when you can ask him to sit – before you put his collar and lead on, before putting his food bowl down and when opening the door to visitors.

1 Call your dog to you. Show him a treat you are holding in your hand and let him sniff at it, but don't allow him to eat it.

2 Move the hand holding the treat slowly back and up, over his head. As his nose moves upwards following the treat, his back end should lower into a sitting position.

If your dog is reluctant to sit

If he tries to jump up instead of sitting it may be because you are holding the treat too high.

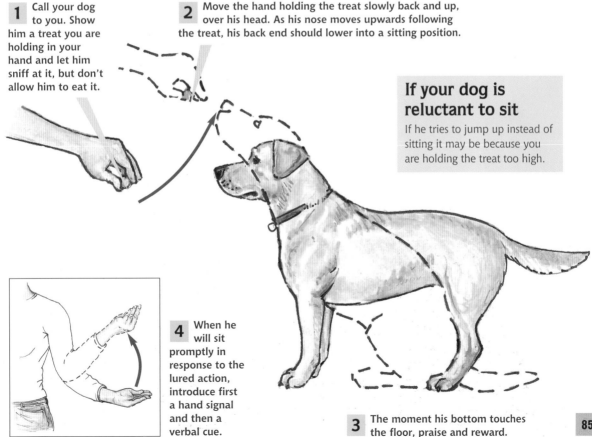

4 When he will sit promptly in response to the lured action, introduce first a hand signal and then a verbal cue.

3 The moment his bottom touches the floor, praise and reward.

85

Teaching 'Down'

1 Ask your dog to sit. Show him a treat held in your hand and allow him to sniff but not eat it.

2 Hold it just in front of his nose and slowly move it downwards and slightly forwards.

4 When he will lie down promptly in response to the lured action, introduce first a hand signal and then a verbal one.

If your dog is reluctant to lie down

Sit on the ground with one or both knees drawn up. Use the treat to lure your dog under the gap formed by your legs so that he has to lie down to reach the treat.

3 As his front end moves down to the ground, praise and reward.

TIP Teach your dog to lie down from a standing position once he's learned how to do it from sit.

Teaching 'Stand'

2 Take a step backwards, at the same time slowly drawing your hand back towards you, keeping the treat level with and just in front of your dog's nose.

1 Ask your dog to sit or lie down. Show him and let him sniff at a treat you are holding in your hand, but don't allow him to have it yet.

3 As his nose follows the treat, the rest of his body will follow and he'll stand up. Praise and reward.

4 When he will stand promptly in response to the lured action, introduce first a hand signal and then a verbal cue.

If your dog is reluctant to stand

- Teach from the 'sit' before trying it from the 'down' position, as this will be easier.
- When teaching 'stand' from the 'down' position, move the treat upwards as well as forwards.

Teaching 'Stay'

This exercise can help keep your dog safe, whether it's because you want him to wait before jumping out of the car or when you open the front door, or to ensure you are in control of his movements when crossing roads. Teach this exercise in easy steps.

If your dog is reluctant to stay

If your dog gets up and tries to follow you, quietly return him to his place and ask him to sit again. Next time, move a little more slowly, or less far away from him, or for a shorter time.

TIP Practise around the house and garden, and out on walks too, gradually increasing the number of distractions until you have a really reliable stay.

2 Ask your dog to sit as before. Take a step to the side away from him and then back to his side. Praise and reward.

1 Ask your dog to sit, but wait for a count of five before praising and rewarding. Gradually increase the amount of time until he will remain in the sit for up to 30 seconds.

3 When he remains happily in the sit, take a step to the side, count to five and then step back beside him. Praise and reward. Once he realizes you want him to stay where he is, use a hand signal and give the verbal cue 'Stay'.

4 Slowly increase the number of steps you take to two, then three and more. Gradually also increase the length of time you are away from his side.

5 Vary the exercise by taking steps forwards and backwards as well. Raise the difficulty not only by increasing distance and duration but by walking a circle around your dog, eventually building up to walking just out of sight. Reaching this point may take a lot of time and practice: don't rush it.

Teaching 'Off' or 'Leave'

This is a very useful exercise. Once learned, it can be used to stop him from stealing food, scavenging, grabbing hold of his lead, or chasing joggers and cyclists. It can also enable you to withdraw from an unwanted encounter with another dog or a similar situation.

1 Hold a piece of food between finger and thumb. Offer it palm uppermost and let your dog take it. Repeat five or six times. Use a fairly low-value treat.

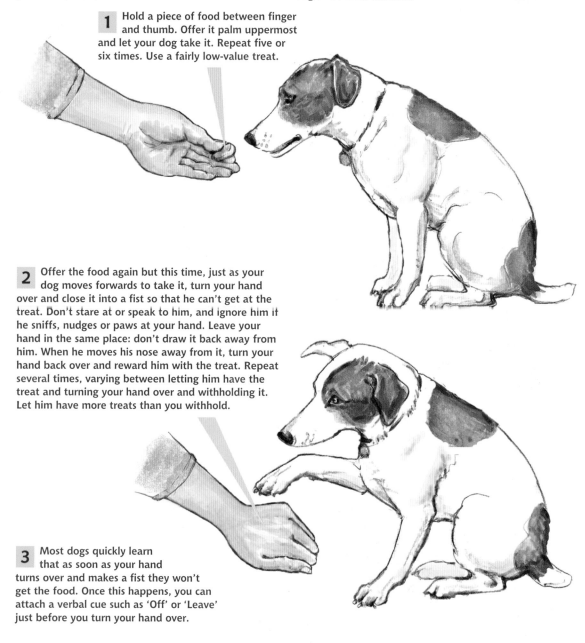

2 Offer the food again but this time, just as your dog moves forwards to take it, turn your hand over and close it into a fist so that he can't get at the treat. Don't stare at or speak to him, and ignore him if he sniffs, nudges or paws at your hand. Leave your hand in the same place: don't draw it back away from him. When he moves his nose away from it, turn your hand back over and reward him with the treat. Repeat several times, varying between letting him have the treat and turning your hand over and withholding it. Let him have more treats than you withhold.

3 Most dogs quickly learn that as soon as your hand turns over and makes a fist they won't get the food. Once this happens, you can attach a verbal cue such as 'Off' or 'Leave' just before you turn your hand over.

4 Once he will leave a lower-value treat, try increasing the tastiness of the food.

5 Try variations of the exercise, such as placing a treat on the floor and partially covering it with your foot to prevent his getting it. When he moves back, reward him with a different treat from your hand.

TIP If you need to put this into practice in a real-life situation, call him to you and be lavish with praise and a treat so he knows he has done the right thing. If you ignore him once he has left the item or distraction he will soon stop responding to you.

Teaching 'Give'

Teaching your dog to surrender an object he has hold of is important, as sometimes it may be necessary to take something away from him that is valuable or dangerous. If he won't let go of a toy, it will also make some games difficult. Teach your dog that it is more rewarding to give up the object than to keep it.

1 Offer your dog a Tuggy-type toy and have a short game with him.

2 When you want him to give up the toy, draw it in close towards you and keep it as still as possible so that the game suddenly becomes less exciting.

3 Offer him a tasty treat with your other hand. In order to take it he'll have to let go of the toy.

If your dog doesn't want to give up the toy

- Put him on a leash so he doesn't learn that he can retain possession by running away from you.
- Make sure the reward you are offering is exciting and tempting enough to make giving up his possession worthwhile.

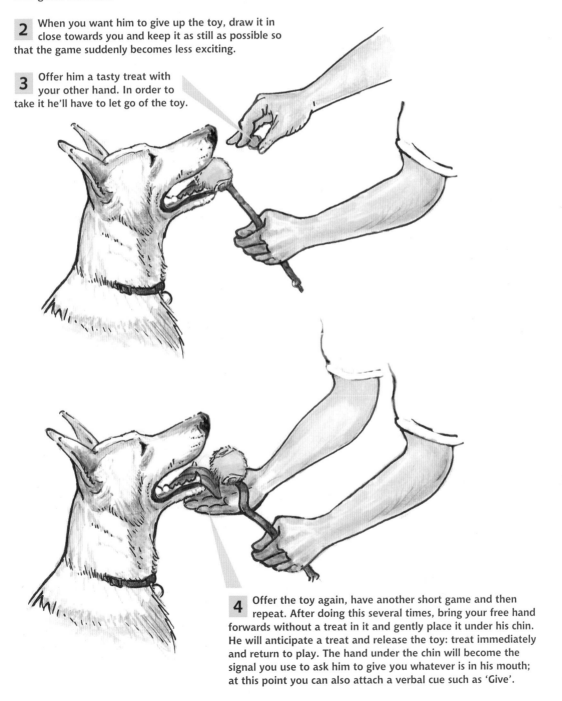

4 Offer the toy again, have another short game and then repeat. After doing this several times, bring your free hand forwards without a treat in it and gently place it under his chin. He will anticipate a treat and release the toy: treat immediately and return to play. The hand under the chin will become the signal you use to ask him to give you whatever is in his mouth; at this point you can also attach a verbal cue such as 'Give'.

Learning to walk on a leash

Walking quietly on a slack leash is an exercise that many owners and dogs never seem to get to grips with. A dog who pulls is not only tiring for you, but could lead to one or both of you getting injured or to your dog pulling free and running off.

1 Hold the leash in one hand so that it is across the front of your body. Use a treat in your other hand to lure your dog into position on that side. When he is standing next to you, facing in the same direction and with the leash hanging with a little slack in it, praise and reward with the treat.

2 Show your dog you have another treat, then take a step forwards with the foot closest to him, using the treat to encourage him to move forwards by your side. After a couple of steps, give him the treat and stop.

3 Repeat, taking just a few steps each time and praising him while the leash remains slack. Over several sessions, gradually increase the number of steps you take to a few yards, then the length of your garden, then a circuit of it. Don't feel you have to keep going once he is on the move: lots of stops and starts will help him learn to balance better so he is less likely to pull and will also give you lots of opportunities for praising and rewarding him.

Common problems

- **If he tries to dash forwards or pull:** stop, keeping your hand in the same position. Attract his attention, use a treat to lure him back into position beside you with the leash slack (see drawing right), praise and reward, then continue as above. Alternatively, try to make a quick change of direction as you walk so that he has to turn and catch up with you. Keep making unpredictable changes of direction so that he has to concentrate on where you are going next.
- **If he tries to chew or bite the leash:** spray the leash with an anti-chew spray (see page 47) and teach a 'Leave' command (see page 88).
- **If he hangs back:** tap the side of your leg and use a treat to coax him forwards. Praise and reward the moment he does. If he is small, make sure you are not going too fast. Never drag your dog along as this is likely to encourage him to pull back more.

Using a harness

A harness will give you greater control if your dog should leap forwards or sideways unexpectedly and reduces the risk of injury to his neck. If later on you want to use only a collar, use a double-ended leash (one with a trigger clip at each end): attach one end to the harness and the other to his collar, and hold it with both hands. This will accustom him to the feel of the leash on his collar and make the transition from the harness easier.

TIP Teach your dog to walk on both your left and right, as there may be times when it's more convenient for him to be on one side than the other.

TIP Keep praising him while the leash remains slack.

Practise your recalls until they are both quick and reliable in all situations.

Teaching a recall

Owners often struggle with this more than with any other exercise. The secret to achieving a good recall is to make it fun and highly rewarding for your dog to return to you.

1 Begin this exercise around your house and garden, as it will be a less distracting environment. Walk a few feet away from your dog, show him that you have a treat, call his name and say 'come'.

2 When your dog arrives, praise and reward him. Feed him tiny pieces of high-value treats for 30 seconds so that he feels it has really been worth coming to you. This will also discourage him from grabbing a treat and running away again: he'll stay close to you to get the next one.

3 Practise as many times a day as possible, and in a variety of places. As he becomes better, call him when you are out of sight – indoors from the garden or from one room to another.

4 When you start teaching your dog away from home, begin in quiet areas with few distractions. Use a long line clipped to a non-tightening harness until you are confident that he will return when you call him.

5 Until the exercise is thoroughly established and his response is virtually automatic, call him only when you are certain he will respond. If he's intent on something else, wait until he's lost interest in it before you call.

TIP No matter how long it takes for your dog to come back to you, never tell him off when he eventually returns, otherwise he'll be even more wary of approaching you the next time.

If your dog is reluctant to come back

- If he has learned to ignore a recall command, go back to teaching him around the house and garden using a different cue word.
- Make sure rewards are sufficiently exciting and desirable.
- Make yourself the most exciting person in the world to be with so that your dog is happy to leave other temptations and come when you want. Call him for a game, or to have a fuss made, as well as for treats. Avoid calling him when you want to do things that he considers less pleasant, such as having his nails clipped.
- Don't call him only when a walk has come to an end. Call him several times during it, praising and rewarding with treats or play and then releasing him to play again.

Make it rewarding for your dog to come back to you by offering a treat or extra-exciting game.

Chapter 5

FUN WITH YOUR DOG

Owning a dog brings lots of responsibilities – and having fun with your pet is one of them. A good relationship is built on mutual respect, communication, tolerance, affection, trust, confidence and acceptance. Making that special connection and developing it over the years involves interacting in a variety of ways. Feeding, grooming, exercising and training all play an important part, but so does having fun, whether it's taking long walks or going jogging, learning new skills or refining old ones, or simply playing games together.

All the activities you do with your dog will strengthen the bond between you, but it's important to match them to his temperament and personality as well as to yours. Unless you choose carefully, they may not have the positive effect you intended, but may make him physically and emotionally uncomfortable instead.

TOYS FOR YOUR D

Choosing and buying a new toy as a present for your dog is fun, bu...
frivolous indulgence. Toys are a necessity as well as a luxury: they ca...
act as training aids, increase your dog's level of exercise and help discou...
behaviour problems, as well as offering different ways for you to play wit...

What sort of toys?

Toys come in all shapes and sizes and are made from a variety of materials. Some are good for chasing and retrieving, others for tug-of-war-type games, others for chewing or to provide mental stimulation. Buy a selection so that you have something suitable for any occasion.

- Buy toys made specifically for dogs and suitable for the activity they are to be used for. Always supervise games with less robust toys made from fabric or latex.
- Remove toys that show signs of wear and tear.
- Don't throw hard rubber balls directly at or to your dog to catch. Make sure all balls are too big to be swallowed. The safest are those with a rope threaded through the centre; these can also be used for tugging games and you will be able to throw them further. Ball-launchers can be fun, but can involve a lot of fast running which may be too much for some dogs.
- Do not allow your dog to share a child's toys. Always supervise play between dogs and children.
- Never throw sticks as they can splinter and perforate the mouth, throat and gut, and injuries can be fatal.
- Don't expect dogs to share toys containing food.
- Don't use toys as a substitute for your company and attention.

How do I keep him interested?

Don't allow your dog to have all his toys at once: leave just a few out and put the rest away. Rotating them on a fortnightly basis will keep them fresh and interesting to him.

If you want to use a toy as a training aid, find the one he likes best of all and get it out for short but exciting games, then put it away out of your dog's sight and reach while he still wants to continue playing. This will help increase its appeal for him and make it a more effective way of motivating him when training.

Invent your own games

Make up your own games. For example, fill a large cardboard box with balls of crumpled newspaper, show your dog a treat, then hide it in the box and invite him to find it. You can also ask him to find treats hidden under a towel, low chair, upturned box or plastic beaker: he'll have to use a different technique with each to retrieve the treat.

A multi-purpose toy

Kongs are very popular toys, versatile as w...
tough. Used as a throwing toy, the erratic...
keep your dog guessing which way it will go...
tightly with food and treats to tease out, it wil... keep
him amused when left on his own.

What if he won't give a toy back?

If your dog is reluctant to surrender a toy, don't get involved in a battle: teach a 'Give' command (see page 89) instead. If he tries to keep possession by running off with it, don't chase after him as this will become another sort of game. Clip a long line on to him and put your foot on it as he starts to move off so that he can't run away. Offer a different toy or a really tasty treat and encourage him to come back to you: use the 'Give' command, then make returning even more rewarding by continuing the game.

TIP Always be the one to initiate and end play sessions. Stop while your dog still wants more and also if he gets over-excited or begins ripping a toy apart.

GOING ON HOLIDAY

re going away, try to ensure that the break is as enjoyable for your dog as it is for you, whether he is coming with you or you are making alternative arrangements for him.

Where to stay with your dog

These days dogs are welcomed in many campsites, B&Bs, self-catering lets and hotels. Take into account your dog's needs: old dogs, or those with fine coats, chill easily and may not enjoy the rigours of camping. Book all accommodation in advance and enquire about any restrictions on height, breed or number of dogs you can take.

The more you plan ahead, the more successful your holiday will be. Check with tourist information centres and online for local walks, dog-friendly pubs and places of interest where your pet can accompany you.

TIP Whenever you are travelling, make sure your dog has water available and ensure he has regular opportunities to stretch his legs and relieve himself.

Holiday etiquette

- On arrival, check where your dog is allowed to go and where you can dispose of poop bags.
- Don't allow your dog to rush up to other guests or their pets.
- Keep your dog off beds and furniture.
- Never leave your dog alone in your room.
- If you are camping, take measures to ensure your dog is kept secure at night.
- Keep your dog on the leash anywhere you don't know well.

What to take

Pack everything you will need for your dog in a separate hold-all rather than mixing it up with your own things. Take:

- Collar with ID and leash. Make sure his ID has a holiday contact number where you can be reached. If he isn't microchipped (see page 72) it's a good idea to get it done before you go.
- Food. A change in diet could upset his stomach. If you are not confident that you can buy your dog's usual food, it is wise to take with you enough to last for the whole holiday.
- First aid kit (see page 114) and any medications your dog takes.
- Towels for drying wet muddy coats and paws.
- Grooming kit.
- Water and food bowls.
- A few toys.
- Bedding. This will help your dog feel more settled at night.
- Poop bags.
- Torch. For late-night strolls for your dog to relieve himself.
- Odour-removing spray and roll of kitchen towel in case he has a toilet accident – it can happen in strange surroundings.
- Details of the local veterinary practice in case of emergency.

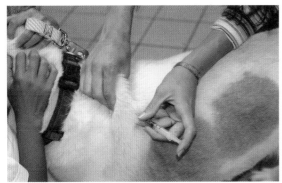

Your dog will need a rabies vaccination if you plan to take him abroad.

Travelling abroad

In the UK the Pet Travel Scheme (PETS) means you can take your dog abroad – but there are some important things to consider:

- Is your pet healthy enough to undertake a journey that could be quite stressful?
- If you are going somewhere hot, will he be able to cope with the temperatures?
- Might he be exposed to potentially fatal diseases not normally found in the UK (e.g. leishmaniasis, caused by the bite of sand flies and prevalent in southern Mediterranean countries)? Have you researched how to prevent him catching these and what to do if you spot symptoms?

PET PASSPORTS

If you travel abroad and don't want your dog quarantined for six months on your return, you will need to apply for a PETS Passport. This can be done through your vet and will require that your dog:

- Is first microchipped (see page 72).
- Is then vaccinated against rabies (see page 73).
- Has a blood test about 30 days after vaccination to ensure it has worked.

The Passport becomes valid six months after the successful blood test result. One or two days before you bring your dog back into the UK from an approved country you will have to:

- Treat your dog for parasites.
- Ensure you have the appropriate documentation for passport control. If this is incomplete or if your dog has not been properly treated for ticks and tapeworm (see pages 112–113), or if the microchip is unreadable, he may be quarantined.

Always check before you go which countries are currently included in the PETS scheme. Some countries may require additional health certificates or import permits and you should be aware of any legislation that affects your dog. Remember that this may vary between regions within countries. It is also advisable to check that your insurance policy offers cover for travel abroad.

Leaving your dog in kennels

If you are not taking your dog on holiday, you will need to make arrangements for his care. Details of boarding kennels can be found in Yellow Pages, telephone directories, canine-interest magazines or from your vet, and other owners may be able to offer personal recommendations. Visit before making a booking, as kennels can vary widely from very basic to luxurious pet hotels. As you look around, you need to consider:

- Are living areas clean, warm, dry, draught-free and well maintained?
- Do staff seem friendly, interested and knowledgeable?
- Do the dogs seem healthy and happy?
- Is the kennel licensed and insured?
- Are only vaccinated dogs accepted, to reduce the risk of disease being transmitted?
- What will happen should your dog become ill?
- How much exercise will your dog receive, and will it be walking on a leash or free running in a safe area?
- Can you supply your own food if you wish? If medication is needed, are staff happy to give it? And if your dog needs grooming, will staff do it?

If you like the kennels, book in plenty of time and, when you take your dog, leave an emergency contact number, plus your pet's bedding, a few toys, any food and medications, and a T-shirt or something that smells of you to comfort him.

Alternative holiday care

Dogs who are elderly or suffer separation anxiety (see page 106) may find a stay in kennels stressful. Consider leaving your pet with a friend or relative, or engaging a 'petsitter' to live in your house and care for your pet during your absence. In addition to your dog remaining in familiar surroundings with plenty of attention, your house will be more secure. Make sure you obtain references, and check if the sitter is a member of any registry and has criminal-record clearances. You should also arrange for the sitter to meet your dog in advance to make sure they get on.

Not all dogs will be happy in kennels, so you may need to make alternative arrangements.

DAYS OUT WITH YOUR DOG

It can be fun to venture a little farther afield than your walks normally take you and enjoy a whole day out with your dog. Exploring new areas will be exciting for him, with new sights and smells to investigate.

Plan your route

Decide in advance where you want to go and work out a suitable route. Be realistic about the distance you can both comfortably cover and remember to allow adequate time for both of you to rest.

It's best for your dog if you choose cooler times of year to go on such outings. Build up his fitness and toughen up his pads in preparation by increasing his exercise at home.

See page 71 for a list of things to take on a walk.

Keep your dog hydrated

Carry water with you and offer it to your dog frequently during the day, as he won't have his usual free access to a water bowl. A collapsible bowl or combined bottle and bowl will be easy to carry. Don't allow him to drink from puddles or streams as they may be contaminated.

Beach walks

The beach is a popular destination for a day out – but check it is dog-friendly before you go, as many are off limits during all or part of the year.

On the beach, follow usual safety precautions, observe warnings and keep a close eye on your dog, as there can be a surprising number of potential hazards, including:
- Other beach-users – anglers, boats, jet-skis, horse riders, kite-fliers, kite-powered craft and, sometimes, cars.
- Cliff edges – can be crumbly and unstable, so keep your dog on a leash when near them.
- Tides – take care that you and your dog don't get cut off by the incoming tide when exploring coves and caves.
- Sand – the beach may look inviting, but watch out for rubbish washed ashore by the sea or left by others, as it could be harmful to your dog. Deep or loose sand can also be very tiring for your dog to run on. Steer well clear of areas known to have sinking sand.

If you are planning to take your dog out on a boat, kit him out with a flotation jacket (available online and from marine stores) in case he falls or jumps overboard. It will make him easier to spot as well as keeping him afloat.

Swimming can be very tiring, so don't allow your dog to overdo things, even though he may be keen to do more. Don't play too many retrieving games as he'll swallow sea water fetching his toy, which can cause retching, vomiting and diarrhoea. Discourage him from swimming too far out from the shore in case he gets into difficulties. Take plenty of towels to dry him so he doesn't get chilled. Rinse out his coat afterwards with clean fresh water, as salt and sand can irritate skin.

SHOWING YOUR DOG

Showing your dog can be an enjoyable way of learning more about the breed you own and of meeting other people with a similar interest. Even if you don't own a registered pedigree, you can still enjoy the fun of showing.

Getting started

A good way of starting out and deciding if this is something you and your dog will enjoy together is to enter a Companion Dog Show. These generally have classes specifically for pedigree dogs as well as novelty classes.

If you do decide to take part in classes at breed shows, your dog will need to be registered with the Kennel Club. You may also find it helpful to become a member of your breed club, and the breeder of your dog may be willing to give you advice. Even if you have attended obedience classes, you'll benefit from joining a club that specializes in ringcraft classes. These will teach you how to present your dog for the judge, and can be good preparation for the 'real thing'.

Visiting shows as a spectator will give you an idea of what is involved, as well as the chance to pick up tips from watching and chatting to exhibitors. You may find that it is not quite as simple as it looks. As well as having a dog who conforms to the description for his individual breed standard, there is a skill in getting him to move and stand well, and to bringing out the best in him so that he catches the eye.

Companion Dog Shows

These shows cater for all dogs, pedigree or mongrel, with a variety of classes such as Prettiest Bitch, Handsomest Dog, Best Veteran, Best Six Legs, Scruffiest Dog, Best Trick and many others.

These shows are generally very popular and make a relaxed, fun day out where your dog will not only be welcome, but will be one of the star attractions. As well as the classes, there are often plenty of other things to see and do, including 'have-a-go' agility and obedience rings.

Giving something back

If you have some spare time on a regular basis and your dog is friendly and not too boisterous, there are many who would greatly appreciate his company. Therapeutic visits by dogs to hospitals, hospices, nursing and care homes, special needs schools and other venues are often the highlight of the week for patients and residents, lifting spirits and giving great pleasure. All sizes and types, pedigrees, crossbreeds and mongrels are welcome to apply to become 'PAT' (Pets As Therapy) dogs: see page 126 for contact details.

Companion Dog Shows usually have classes for both pedigree and non-pedigree dogs and can be a fun day out.

COMPETITIVE SKILLS AND SPORTS

It is important to keep up your dog's training, and once he has mastered the basics there are lots of different ways you can do this, whether purely for pleasure, to work off surplus energy or to enjoy the fun and challenges of competing together.

Fun with your dog

Obedience

If you enjoyed teaching basic obedience to your dog (see Chapter 4), you may like to try to take things a little further, learning new skills, polishing old ones and perhaps testing what you both know in competition.

Starting with pre-beginners' classes, there are six levels of competitive obedience, with exercises ranging from heelwork (the dog walking close to his handler's leg) on and off the leash, sits and stays of different duration, and scent discrimination (sniffing out a specific article from among several others). Joining a club that specializes in obedience training will help you get off to a good start.

Rally Obedience

Also known as Rally-O, this competition was devised by the American Kennel Club and recently introduced to the UK by the Association of Pet Dog Trainers (APDT). It includes an element of agility (see page 100) as well as obedience, and any dog with a basic level of training can take part.

Competitors progress at their own pace around a series of 'stations' with signs giving instructions for the skill to be performed at each. These include movements such as left and right turns, U-turns, about-turns, sit-down-sit, figure of eight, and send away and recall over a low hurdle.

Find out more about Rally-O by contacting the APDT in the UK or the American Kennel Club in the US.

Obedience competitions give you a chance to test your skills.

Heelwork to Music

This relatively new canine sport involves devising a routine with your dog and setting it to music. It includes two categories – Heelwork to Music (HTM), which involves the dog remaining close to the handler at all times; and Freestyle, which allows a greater range of imaginative movements. Freestyle is particularly popular with spectators as well as competitors, and is a combination of obedience, trick training, theatrical flair and musical choreography. Moves performed by your dog during a routine might include weaving in and out of your legs, standing up, crawling, rolling over, reversing and jumping through your arms.

Even if you don't want to compete, the variety of skills involved – including changes of direction and speed, as well as learning new exercises – can be a stimulating challenge and an enjoyable change from traditional obedience work.

You can find out more about getting started in HTM by contacting the Kennel Club.

Trick training

If even Heelwork to Music is too formal for you but you'd like to continue teaching your dog new skills, consider teaching tricks instead. These can vary from simple – shaking a paw – to more difficult, such as putting named toys in a box or bringing a hanky when you sneeze. Clicker training (see page 82) can be helpful in building up steps in more complex sequences of actions. Some tricks can serve a practical purpose too: rolling over or offering a paw can make it easier to groom, for example.

Good Citizen Dog Scheme

Originally devised by the American Kennel Club, there are now Good Citizen Dog Schemes, run along similar lines, in the UK and many other European countries. It is the largest dog-training scheme in the UK and over 80,000 dogs have successfully passed the tests since its inception in 1992.

What Is It?

The scheme aims to:
- Promote responsible dog ownership.
- Enhance your relationship with your pet.
- Make others in the community more aware of the benefits of dog ownership.

The course consists of a structured series of tests which encourage you to increase your knowledge and to achieve certain levels of training with your dog. Success must be achieved at the most basic level before you can proceed to the next. Any dog of any age, breed or type can participate.

What Happens?

There are Bronze, Silver and Gold A... requires you to pass 10 different exercis... dog's training but also your own theoretica... of subjects relating to his care, such as diet, hea... the responsibilities of ownership. The requirements ... Bronze, but become increasingly more challenging as y... through the other levels. All the exercises have to be compl... satisfactorily in order to pass, and in the event of re-taking a te... will have to complete and pass all the sections again, not just the one previously deemed 'not ready'.

Awards for Puppies

Puppies can also take part in the Good Citizen Dog Scheme. The Puppy Foundation Assessment is based on continuous assessment of owner and dog at training classes rather than by a formal test. During this time both are assessed on 12 different exercises, including care, cleanliness, puppy play, response to name, socialization, puppy recall, walking in a controlled way and food manners.

Working Towards an Award

If you are doing the Puppy Foundation Assessment, then you will need to join a course, but if you wish you can work towards the other levels yourself. In order to prepare properly, however, many owners do find it helpful to join a club or enrol on a course: contact the Kennel Club for details (see page 126).

The Kennel Club's Good Citizen Award Scheme offers goals to aim for with your pet.

...first public appearance in 1978 at Crufts Dog Show, this sport has gone from strength to strength to become the fastest-growing canine sport in the UK, Western Europe and the USA. Although lots of owners enjoy competing with their pet, just as many do it purely for fun.

WHAT IS IT?

Agility combines elements of obedience and athleticism. It is also a great bonding activity, developing trust, confidence, observation and communication between dog and handler. Your dog jumps over, runs along or goes through a variety of obstacles, including:

- Hurdles.
- A-frame.
- Tyre.
- Long jump.
- Rigid and collapsible tunnels.
- Dog walk.
- Seesaw.
- Table.
- Weave poles.

HOW TO GET STARTED

Anyone can take part, young or old. Although a reasonable amount of handler fitness is an asset, there have been successful disabled handlers. Dogs should be reasonably fit and not overweight, and must be at least 12 months old, or older in the case of slow-maturing breeds. Standard equipment may not be suitable for giant breeds. You will need to:

- Have taught basic obedience to your dog and have good control of him. This is important for his safety as well as to enable you to progress.
- Use a flat collar and fixed leash until your dog is ready to work off the leash.
- Wear sensible clothes that won't restrict your movement, and shoes suitable for running. Avoid baggy sleeves which can obscure hand signals.
- Have treats or a toy to use as rewards for your dog while he is learning.
- Join a club or enrol on a course: this will provide safe, properly constructed obstacles and teach you the right way of tackling them safely.

A poor introduction risks injury to your pet and loss of his confidence.

COMPETING

As you become more proficient, you may decide to compete. Courses generally consist of around 16–20 obstacles with penalties incurred for errors such as knocking down a hurdle or missing one of the 'contact' points which your dog is required to touch with his paws. The winner is the dog who completes the course in the fastest time with no penalties.

Classes are divided into different levels to suit all abilities and sizes of dogs. Many offer rosettes for clear rounds as well as placings, so even if your dog isn't very fast you still stand a chance of winning a ribbon.

Agility can be a fun way for you and your dog to interact with each other.

If you have an active dog who likes to chase balls, flyball may be just the sport for him.

Flyball

Fast and furious, this sport is as exciting for spectators as for the dogs taking part. Two teams of four dogs compete against each other at the same time. One dog from each team is sent away over a line of four hurdles, at the end of which is a special flyball box. The dog presses a pedal on the box to release a tennis ball into the air, which the dog catches and then returns with it down the line of hurdles to the handler. The next dog is then sent off until all four have gone. The first team to have their fourth dog cross the finish line wins and usually the best of three runs decides which team goes on to the next heat.

If you think this is an activity your dog might enjoy, it's best to join a club that specializes in this form of competition.

Cani-cross

Many owners enjoy jogging with their dogs for pleasure as well as to keep fit and now it's possible to do it competitively in the form of canine cross-country or 'cani-cross'. Races are most often held over a distance of 5 km, but 10 km and 21 km events are also held, as well as shorter 'have-a-go' courses covering 2.5 km.

Runners and dogs set off individually at intervals, following a set course across country. There are no time limits, so you can go at your own (and your dog's) pace. No special equipment is needed beyond what you would normally wear for running, although you should remember to take poop bags with you and clear up after your dog. If you find that you get hooked on the sport, invest in a special running belt and harness and a stretchy bungee leash. This will make it easier for you and takes all pressure off your dog's neck so his breathing isn't restricted and he doesn't receive any sudden jerks from the leash. Teaching verbal commands for turning left, right, stopping and overtaking others will help you let your dog know what to do without having to touch him.

As with any exercise programme, make sure that both you and your dog have a health check first and gradually build up the duration of exercise as you prepare for events.

Another sport you might like to try is 'caniteering', which combines running and orienteering with your dog.

Specialist activities

Many breeds were originally bred to do a particular job. If you own one of these canine 'specialists', you might find it fun to try your hand at an activity which relates to this. Contact the breed club to find out activities for which your dog may be eligible, including:

Bloodhound Trials. Bloodhounds follow a human scent trail, ignoring all other distractions, and at the end are asked to pick out from a line-up the runner who laid the trail.

Field Trials and Gundog Working Trials. These are designed to test the working ability of gundogs, so simulate as closely as possible a typical day's shooting.

Sheepdog training. If you have a herding dog you don't need to be a shepherd or farmer to develop and give an outlet to his innate instincts – there are many sheepdog schools and courses you can attend together.

Sleddog racing. A winter sport for Arctic breeds – but if conditions are snowless, traditional sledges are exchanged for chariot-type wheeled vehicles called rigs.

Working Trials. These are a competitive civilian equivalent of police work, with exercises that include following scents and recovering items, negotiating high and wide obstacles, heelwork, retrieving objects and recalls.

TIP Many country shows offer the chance to have a go at events such as agility, terrier racing and dock diving (a long jump into water). They may also have Companion Dog Shows, and can be a good source of information on canine pursuits.

Chapter 6

BEHAVIOUR PROBLEMS

Should you experience any behaviour problems with your dog, they are unlikely to vanish of their own accord. The longer you leave matters, the more established and harder to change they will become.

If you are considering taking on a rescue dog with a known behaviour problem, bear in mind that, although love is important, it is not sufficient by itself. Make sure you feel confident enough and have sufficient time, patience, commitment and resources to cope. You should also check that you will be able to rely on the shelter for advice and support while working through the difficulty.

The causes of some behaviour problems are very obvious and may be simple to remedy. Others, however, may be more complex, involving multiple factors such as diet, exercise, training, previous experiences and daily routine, all of which will need addressing. Solutions may also need careful tailoring to the individual dog and owner – what is applicable to one may not necessarily be appropriate for another – and with some a complete 'cure' may never be feasible.

With any behaviour problem it is always important first to ask your vet to examine your dog, as physical problems can frequently be either a main or a contributory cause. If you are unable to cope with a problem, are making no progress with it, or it is something outside your experience, seek professional help: ask your vet to refer you to a pet behaviour counsellor or trainer.

Aggression of any sort can be a serious problem for which you should seek professional help as soon as possible.

Aggression

Aggression towards people or other dogs is the most common problem for which people seek professional help. Causes may range from fear to physical pain and hormonal imbalances, but whatever the underlying reason, such behaviour can be very frightening and potentially injurious, even fatal. Do not try to solve the problem on your own, but seek expert help as soon as possible.

If your dog shows any signs of aggression:

1. Stay calm.
2. Be as neutral as possible. Do not be confrontational, as this is likely to provoke further aggressive behaviour.
3. Remove him from the situation as calmly as possible.
4. Contact your vet and ask him to give your dog a thorough physical examination and, if necessary, a referral to a pet behaviour counsellor.
5. In the meantime avoid situations likely to trigger a reactive response and keep him on the lead and muzzled at all times when in public. Consider carefully whether any risk is posed to family members.

Attention seeking

Dogs can sometimes become a bit excessive in their demands for food, a toy or affection, and may:

- Bark, howl or whine.
- Jump up at you.
- Grab your hand or clothing.
- Stare at you.

It is instinctive to scold or push your dog away, but from his point of view any attention is better than none at all, so his actions have paid off. Make them counterproductive by withdrawing your attention, turning away from him or leaving the room. As soon as he is quiet, call him to you, ask him to do something (even if just a simple 'sit' exercise) and praise and reward him. This allows you to control interaction and shows him he has to earn your attention rather than being able to demand and receive it whenever he pesters.

Barking

A dog who barks loudly for any length of time is often unhappy and distressed. Barking can be a major source of annoyance to neighbours and, if a complaint is made, could lead to your being prosecuted (see also page 73).

Why dogs bark

- Confusion – not understanding what you want when training. Check you are giving clear verbal and physical cues, go back a few steps if necessary, and ensure that your dog is physically able to perform the task.
- Attention seeking – see left.
- Boredom when left on his own – especially if under-exercised and lacking mental stimulation. Increasing the quantity and quality of exercise and leaving an activity toy such as a treat-stuffed Kong to keep him occupied may help. If you need to be absent for any length of time, hire the services of a dogwalker or petsitter, or investigate the possibility of doggy daycare.
- Separation anxiety – see page 106.
- Visual stimulation – if your dog barks at passing dogs or people, draw the curtains, create a screen of foliage or fencing in the garden or confine your dog to a different area.
- Senility or illness – barking can be a symptom of CCD in elderly dogs (see page 123). Brain disturbance due to illness or a tumour may also be responsible. Consult your vet.
- Alarm barking – if your dog alerts you to someone at the door, ask him to sit after a couple of barks. Wait until he stops barking. When he does, say 'hush' and reward him. Ask someone to stand outside and knock on the door or ring the bell so you can practise teaching the 'hush' command more quickly.

Helping your dog stop barking

If your dog barks excessively, do not shout at him – he'll think you are joining in and will bark even more.

- Stay calm.
- Reward quiet behaviour.
- Keep obedience training up to scratch as this can make it easier to resolve some barking issues.

Seek professional help if you are having trouble remedying the problem and reassure your neighbours that you are taking steps to deal with the situation.

Chewing

Chewing is a perfectly normal puppy behaviour – dogs use their mouths much as we use our hands to explore and learn more about objects and the surrounding environment. Discomfort while teething may also lead to increased chewing activity. Keep those areas where your pet is allowed as tidy and clutter-free as possible and use taste-deterrent sprays on areas such as doorframes, chair or table legs which may be targeted. If you catch him chewing something he shouldn't, swap it for a more appropriate object instead, such as a toy or chewy treat.

In adult dogs, chewing can be an enjoyable and absorbing activity, but can also be due to boredom or separation anxiety (see page 106).

Digging

Some dogs love to dig and it can be difficult to prevent, especially in breeds such as terriers for whom it is a part of their heritage. Rather than attempting to stop it completely, encourage digging in a permitted area (see page 50) and protect flowerbeds by laying wire netting or branches on top.

Fear of fireworks or thunder

Fear of fireworks or thunderstorms can sometimes be traced to a bad experience but even pets who have been fine in the past can suddenly become fearful for no apparent reason. Anxiety will often escalate, becoming worse on each successive occasion.

- Introduce a desensitization programme using high-quality sound recordings of fireworks or thunder. Initially these are played at the lowest possible volume during enjoyable activities such as eating and games. It is vital not to rush things and it may take some dogs months rather than weeks to become less afraid of and reactive to the sounds.

- Cuddling your dog can sometimes reinforce rather than allay his fears, making it seem to him that you are anxious too. You can, however, use TTouch (see 'Teach your dog through touch', page 40) as a more positive way of helping to calm, reassure and lower stress levels without sending the wrong messages. Use of close-fitting T-shirts (specially designed for dogs and available from many pet shops) has also produced good results with some dogs.

- Offering a long-lasting treat or stuffed Kong may help distract your dog – and the action of chewing can release stress-relieving endorphins.

- Frightened dogs often try to squeeze into small, dark spaces under or behind furniture. Provide an alternative by placing a blanket over the top of his crate. Leave the door open and allow him to choose whether he wants to go in or not. Alternatively, drape a blanket over two chairs or over a table to make a safe den for him.

- Feed your dog before any disturbances are expected. If possible, include turkey, which is a rich source of tryptophan, and carbohydrates such as pasta or rice which enhance its absorption. Tryptophan is converted into serotonin in the brain, and is involved in sleep, mood and sensitivity, producing feelings of contentment, relaxation and pleasure. Exercise earlier in the day can also increase natural serotonin levels.

- Pull curtains to shut out noises and flashes, make sure cat and dog flaps are securely shut and turn up the TV, radio or sound system loud enough to drown out some of the external noise, although not to an uncomfortable volume.

- A DAP diffuser (see page 45) may have a calming, reassuring effect.

- Herbal remedies based on valerian and skullcap have relaxing and sedative properties which will reduce anxiety levels. Essential oils and homeopathy can prove helpful. Take advice from an experienced practitioner and check with your vet before use if your dog has any known health problems.

Dogs are both natural scavengers and opportunists so may well steal any food left within their reach.

Food stealing

Some dogs just cannot resist any opportunity to steal food. Apart from the problem of your dinner vanishing, this habit can lead to upset stomachs and some foods may be dangerous.

- Teach a 'Leave' command (see page 88).
- Teach your dog to go to his bed at mealtimes so that you aren't pestered for food.
- Keep foodstuffs out of reach if you can't be present in the room; some dogs are expert worktop-surfers with a surprising reach, while others may be agile enough to jump up on work surfaces. Put food away rather than leaving it out, and if necessary fit child locks on cupboard doors.
- Rubbish bins are another temptation for many dogs: make sure he can't flip the lid open or knock the bin over to access the contents. If necessary, buy a bin that fits inside a cupboard or keep it outside.

Jumping up

A puppy who jumps up may be cute while he's still small, but as he grows this behaviour will become less welcome, especially if he has muddy paws or if your hands are full. It can also be intimidating for strangers and knock small children and frail seniors flying.

If your dog jumps up to try to gain attention:

1. Fold your arms, turn away and withhold attention, not speaking to, looking at or touching him.
2. The moment he puts all four feet back on the floor reward with praise and a treat.
3. Remember that pushing him away or telling him off will be rewarding to him (see 'Attention seeking', page 103).

If your dog jumps up in excitement when greeting you or visitors at the door, keep a pot of treats nearby but out of his reach and teach him this door routine:

1. Ask him to sit and stay (see pages 85 and 87) as the door is opened.
2. If he gets up, shut the door, repeat the command to sit and stay, then start again.
3. Ask him to remain sitting as the person comes in, rewarding him by dropping a treat on the floor – this will encourage him to keep his feet on the floor as well as rewarding him for it.

Play biting

Puppies may have tiny teeth, but they are needle sharp and, if they get carried away while playing, a nip or bite can be very painful and even break the skin. You can teach him that this isn't acceptable behaviour by doing exactly what his playmates would do – immediately stop playing and cry out with an expressive 'ow!' Turn away and withdraw your attention for a couple of minutes before calling him and resuming play.

Food guarding

If your dog is protective of food, never try to remove it forcibly while he's eating – this is likely to make him more irritable and to increase his efforts to prevent you from doing so. Puppies can be taught that your presence nearby is to be welcomed (see page 64), but if you have acquired a dog inclined to guard food it may be safer to try a slightly different tactic.

1. Place three empty bowls on the floor at a distance from each other and drop a piece of food in one.
2. While your dog eats it, move on to the next bowl and let him see you drop another piece of food in that. This allows you to keep a safer distance between you until he realizes that you provide rather than remove food and stops viewing you as a threat.
3. With this sort of dog it may be wise not to give bones to chew on. If you have other pets, prevent fights by feeding them in separate rooms and give only treats that can be eaten quickly.

A dog who suffers from separation anxiety will experience genuine mental anguish if left on his own.

Separation anxiety

After aggression, separation anxiety is the most common problem seen by pet behaviour counsellors. It can be stressful for both the dog and for neighbours if he barks or howls.

What is it?

Being left at home can be agonizing for a dog who suffers from separation anxiety. He may become anxious as he sees you getting ready to depart and, once alone, his feelings of panic can escalate and he may display behaviours including:

- Whining, barking, howling.
- Panting, excessive salivation.
- Fouling and/or urinating.
- Destructive behaviour, such as digging, scratching or chewing.
- Self-mutilation.

Some of these behaviours may also be due to other causes: young puppies will chew while teething; both young and old dogs may lack good bladder and bowel control; and under-exercised dogs may run riot when no one is around out of a combination of sheer boredom and an excess of pent-up energy.

Why does it happen?

Dogs who have not been taught early on to be alone (see page 77) or who are overly attached to their owners are most likely to be affected, as well as those who have had a frightening experience, such as hearing a thunderstorm while on their own. Changes in circumstances, such as a house move, a new routine, loss of an animal companion or member of the family can also give rise to problems, as can physical difficulties such as failing eyesight, deafness, arthritis and incontinence.

How do you remedy it?

Resolving separation anxiety will take time and commitment and you will need to.

Arrange for a health check from your vet: investigate any possibility of physical problems.

Lessen his dependence on your physical presence: teach and develop the 'Stay' exercise (see page 87) and teach him to be at a distance from you in the house (see page 77).

Change departure associations: dogs quickly learn to identify and associate with your immediate departure all the things you do before going out and may begin to show increasing anxiety as you prepare to leave. Practise doing all the things you would normally do – picking up keys, putting on your coat and fetching your bag – but then continue with an activity inside so that you change the associations. Progress from this to going to the door as though you were about to leave, opening and shutting it but staying indoors; then to going through the door without shutting it and coming back in; and then to going outside, shutting the door briefly and returning indoors. Gradually extend the time you are outside.

Don't make a fuss: begin to withdraw attention around half an hour before you leave – making a big fuss or having a lengthy goodbye will make your absence more noticeable. Don't leave him in a crate to limit damage, as if he becomes frantic he could injure himself. If he must be confined, it's better to leave him in a room, removing any objects he might damage or hurt himself on. When you return, keep your greeting low key, waiting until he is relaxed and calm, then greet him affectionately but quietly.

Travelling problems

As well as feeling thoroughly miserable, a dog who is unhappy and ill at ease in the car can be a dangerous passenger liable to distract the driver's attention.

How to tell if your dog is unhappy

Behaviours indicating that your dog is not happy in the car can range from mild to extreme and include:
- Whining.
- Drooling.
- Scratching at the interior; restlessness; constantly changing position.
- Jumping around.
- Destructiveness – tearing at the car interior.
- Vomiting.
- Barking.
- Refusing to get in the car.

Understanding the causes

If you can determine why your dog is a bad passenger it will help you work out the best solution. Sometimes there may be more than one reason, so a certain amount of trial and error as well as good observation may be needed. Common causes include:
- A previous bad experience such as an accident, trips to the vet or poor driving can create unpleasant associations and cause even the calmest of dogs to become anxious. Equally, if there are strong associations with always going for a walk at the end of a journey, anticipation and excitement will increase stress levels.
- Poor balance can affect dogs of all ages, not just those who are very young and lack coordination or elderly ones who are less mobile. This will contribute to motion sickness, which can lead to vomiting, which in turn will increase anxiety.
- Discomfort can often be a big contributory factor: seats are not always wide enough to accommodate your dog in a position he finds comfortable, and just as some people feel nauseous when sitting sideways on to the movement, the same can apply to your dog.
- Physical inability may be the cause of any reluctance to get in the car. The car's motion may also increase discomfort in stiff, aching joints.
- Over-stimulation at the sight of things whizzing past the window can be a cause of stress. A dog who is flying from side to side, barking and wagging his tail furiously, is more likely to be anxious than enjoying the ride.

Helping your dog to be a better passenger

- Make travelling by car a familiar routine and not one associated solely with special occasions. At the same time, create pleasant associations with being in the car. See page 78 for advice on this and giving your dog as pleasant a journey as possible.
- Good airflow is important – open a rear window a little.
- Different cars give different rides – in estate cars there is often less airflow at the boot end where the dog usually travels; there is also more swing when turning. Others have harder or softer suspension which will affect both comfort and your dog's ability to balance. Try hiring a car to see if it makes a difference.
- Teaching your dog how to improve his balance often helps considerably. TTouch groundwork (see 'Teach your dog through touch', page 40) can be invaluable for this and the TTouches can be used to calm and reassure anxious passengers. Wearing a fitted dog T-shirt can also help with balance.
- Fill in the footwell if your dog sits on a back seat, so he has the choice of facing forwards if he wishes.
- If your dog travels in a crate, experiment with its position: there may be more vibration and noise if it is over the wheels. Placing it towards or in the centre of the car may make it quieter and reduce swing when turning.
- Fit an anti-sickness static strip (available from car accessories shops) – they are cheap and may help.
- Teach your dog to walk along a ramp if it is physically too hard for him to jump in and out of the car.
- If he becomes overstimulated by seeing passing objects, put him in a crate covered with a sheet so that he can't see out.
- Bach Flower Rescue Remedy can help while working through problems – add 5 drops to your dog's water bowl. Homeopathic remedies may also be helpful. Take advice from an experienced practitioner and consult your vet before use.

Reluctance to get in the car may be due to physical inability or unpleasant associations.

Chapter 7

YOUR DOG'S HEALTH

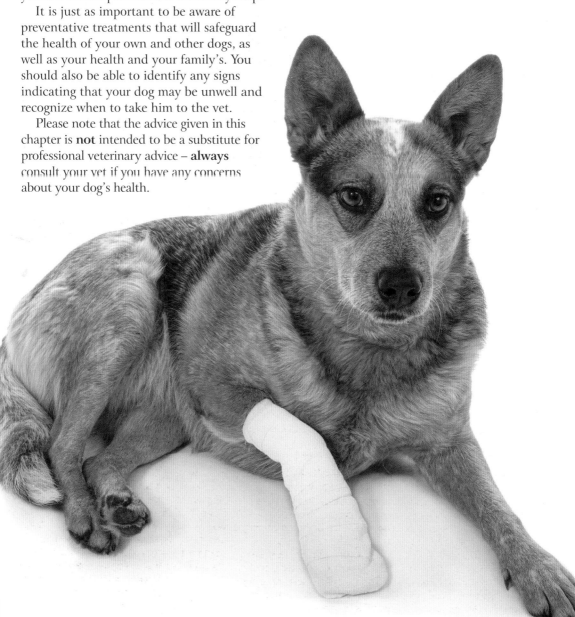

With care, your dog will be healthy as well as happy, but it's impossible to foresee all eventualities. Should he become ill or sustain some kind of accidental injury, a knowledge of basic first aid will help you to deal with minor problems and in an emergency to give appropriate treatment until you can obtain professional veterinary help.

It is just as important to be aware of preventative treatments that will safeguard the health of your own and other dogs, as well as your health and your family's. You should also be able to identify any signs indicating that your dog may be unwell and recognize when to take him to the vet.

Please note that the advice given in this chapter is **not** intended to be a substitute for professional veterinary advice – **always** consult your vet if you have any concerns about your dog's health.

DAILY HEALTH CHECK

The earlier a problem is spotted, the more successful treatment is likely to be. Check your dog over from head to toe every day so that you are familiar with his body and note anything unusual.

1. **Body** – ribs just able to be felt under a thin layer of fat.
2. **Bottom** – anus clean and free of soiling. If you have an unspayed bitch, discharge from the vagina may indicate pyometra, a potentially life-threatening infection (see page 121).
3. **Feet** – nails not split or overlong. No signs of cracking or cuts on the pads, and no grass seeds trapped between the toes.
4. **Coat and skin** – coat clean and without matts, which may build into clumps and pull painfully at the skin. No soiling or patches of hair loss. The skin should move easily over the underlying tissues and feel warm but not hot to the touch. No flaky, itchy or sore areas, and no signs of fleas or ticks (see page 112).
5. **Ears** – clean and pale pink inside. Inflammation, smelly discharges, persistent scratching, head-tilting or head-shaking all indicate a problem.
6. **Eyes** – bright and clear, with both eyelids fully open, not half-closed or blinking rapidly. A tiny amount of 'sleep' in the corner of the eye is natural, but watery or pus-like discharges may indicate an infection. Tear-staining in the corners of the eyes may be due to blocked tear ducts. Membranes of the eyes should be salmon pink in colour.

7. **Nose** – a cold, wet nose is not necessarily a sign of good health, nor does a warm, dry one always indicate illness, but watch out for crusty deposits, clear or pus-coloured discharges or bleeding.
8. **Mouth** – gums moist, free of soreness or bleeding and salmon pink in colour. Paleness may be due to anaemia, a blue tinge to a circulatory problem, and yellowness to jaundice. If the gums are dark-pigmented, check the membranes of the eyes instead. When the ball of a finger is pressed against the gums, they should briefly go pale, then return to normal colour within 1–2 seconds of releasing the pressure. Breath may smell doggy but shouldn't be offensive. Some breeds drool a lot, but none should be salivating or panting heavily.
9. **Lumps and bumps** – note the appearance of any lumps or bumps, including size and texture. Being able to inform your vet of any changes may be helpful to his diagnosis.
10. **Behaviour** – changes in behaviour are often overlooked or dismissed as unimportant, but grumpiness and lack of enthusiasm to play or go for a walk can be signs of pain.
11. **Daily habits** – changes in appetite, drinking, urinating, defecating and sleeping can all indicate the presence of a health problem.

Vital signs

Monitoring vital signs can help you decide if a trip to the vet is needed. They can vary between size and breed, so you need to know what is normal for your dog. Check when he is resting, not after exercise or when he is excited.

Heart and pulse rate: 70–140 beats/minute
How to take it. To feel the heartbeat, place the fingers of one hand on the left side of the chest just under the elbow joint. The easiest pulse to find is the femoral pulse on the inside of the back leg, close to the groin. Don't press too hard or you will stop the blood flow and won't feel the pulse.

Respiratory rate: 10–30 breaths/minute
How to take it. You can normally see the chest moving: count either as it moves up **or** down, but not both. If breathing is very shallow, hold a piece of dry grass or strand of your hair in front of your dog's nostrils and watch it for movement. Note any abnormalities, such as wheezing, gurgling or irregular breaths.

Rectal temperature: 37.8–38.9°C
How to take it. Ask someone to hold your dog if necessary. Use a digital thermometer and lubricate the end with water-soluble jelly. Gently insert the thermometer into the rectum, rotating it slightly as you do so. When the thermometer beeps, gently remove it, read the temperature and then disinfect the thermometer. If your dog really dislikes having his temperature taken and is liable to become fractious or snappy, don't be insistent – leave it to the vet.

GOING TO THE VET

Your dog will need to visit the vet not only if he becomes ill or injured, but for an annual health check and booster vaccinations too. You will also need to take him for routine procedures such as neutering, dental care and advice on dealing with parasites.

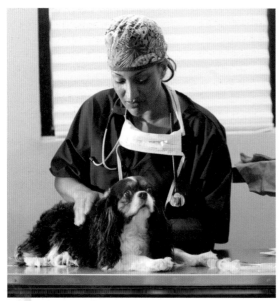

If you have an appointment to take your dog to the vet for surgery, you wil need to withhold food and water for a period of time beforehand. Your vet will advise you about this.

Choosing a vet

Don't wait until your dog needs professional medical help before registering with a vet. Veterinary practices in your area are listed in Yellow Pages; also ask other owners and training clubs for recommendations, or use the 'Find a Vet' service on the Royal College of Veterinary Surgeons (RCVS) website. Making the right choice is important, so visit the practice before registering your pet.

Experience with your breed of dog is an asset and being able to see the same vet each time will ensure continuity of treatment. Good bedside manner is not an indication of expertise but will make visits less stressful for you and your dog. Other points to consider include:

- Is it close enough to get to quickly in an emergency?
- Is the waiting area clean and tidy?
- Are the reception staff friendly and helpful?
- Are there noticeboards with helpful notices and thank-you cards from clients?
- What are the opening times?
- What arrangements are in place if overnight hospitalization is needed?
- How is out-of-hours cover organized?

FEES

Veterinary fees can be very expensive, so consider getting your dog insured (see page 121).

Getting to the surgery

Ensure your dog is safely secured in the back of a car (see page 78). If his illness or injury means you cannot use a harness or crate, get someone to sit with him and hold him on a back seat. If no one is available to do this, place pillows and blankets around him for support.

If you don't have a car and a friend can't help, contact your vet, as they usually keep a list of local taxi services willing to accept dogs as passengers. Public transport is best avoided: it isn't always reliable and could mean an arduous and uncomfortable journey for a sick dog.

At the surgery

Keep your dog under good control when you arrive, as the waiting room may contain a variety of animals. If your pet is very anxious about going to the vet or doesn't get on well with other dogs, wait outside until the vet is ready for you.

Provide as much information as possible about your dog's symptoms, including:

- When they started and if they have altered in severity.
- Your dog's recent activities.
- Any changes in behaviour.
- Change in eating, drinking, urination, bowel movements.

RESTRAINING YOUR DOG

The vet will want to examine your dog, either on the floor or on a table. Never let him jump on or off the table: lift him up and down. It may reassure your dog if you hold him rather than an unfamiliar person, but if you prefer, the vet will call a nurse to assist. Use only as much restraint as is necessary to keep your pet still: too much may make him panic and struggle.

Even the most placid and well-behaved dog may try to bite if frightened or in pain. Your immediate reaction may be to scold but this will only increase his anxiety. Speak reassuringly instead. Don't hold his nose unless asked to do so: it places your hand in a vulnerable position if he snaps.

To ensure that a thorough examination can be carried out safely, it may be necessary to muzzle him; your vet will have a selection of different types and sizes.

Leaving the surgery

After you have seen the vet, make sure that you:

- Collect any medications which have been prescribed, plus instructions for dosage and administration.
- Have been advised about any aftercare.
- Arrange any further appointments.

PREVENTATIVE HEALTH CARE

Prevention is almost always better than cure. It can save your pet suffering unnecessary stress and discomfort, and in some cases may prolong his life.

Vaccination

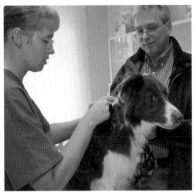

Vaccination reduces the risk of disease to other dogs as well as to your own.

Widespread use of vaccination has done much to reduce the chances of encountering a number of potentially fatal diseases, and many groomers, training classes, dog shows and boarding kennels will not accept dogs unless they are vaccinated. Most vets advise vaccinating against:

- Canine distemper.
- Canine infectious hepatitis.
- Canine parvovirus.
- Leptospirosis.

Your vet may also recommend kennel cough and parainfluenza vaccinations. In some countries a rabies shot is mandatory: your dog will require one if you wish to take him abroad and re-enter the UK (see pages 73 and 95).

Newborn puppies receive some immunity from their mothers but the level of protection becomes minimal by the age of 7–12 weeks, so initial vaccinations are usually given at 8–9 weeks, followed by a second course 2–4 weeks later. After this, 'booster' vaccinations are given at regular intervals: some yearly, others on a three-yearly basis.

Your vet will give you a vaccination certificate recording details of what vaccines have been given and when. Keep it safe, as it is proof when required and reminds you when re-vaccination is due.

Obesity

Around 50 per cent of dogs in the UK and USA are clinically obese (15 per cent over their ideal body weight). Allowing your pet to become overweight reduces his mobility and quality of life. It can also cause many avoidable health problems and contribute to others, and can even shorten his life. In most cases, excess weight stems from a combination of eating too much and exercising too little.

You should just be able to feel his ribs and, when looking at him from above, be able to see a slight inwards dip between the end of his ribcage and his hips. Weigh him on a monthly basis, either by holding him while standing on the bathroom scales, weighing yourself again without him and then subtracting one reading from the other, or by using the scales in your vet's surgery.

Obesity can lead to a number of health problems and shorten your dog's life.

Disease or a prescribed medication may also be responsible for weight gain, so before putting your dog on a diet, always ask your vet to give him a health check. Your vet will also be able to advise on a sensible diet and exercise programme, and on what your dog's optimum weight should be – there are no guidelines for crossbreeds and even pedigrees can vary considerably between individuals. Many practices also run free 'weightwatcher' clinics to help you follow up the advice.

Neutering

Although any operation involves a degree of risk, neutering is a relatively safe procedure. As well as stopping behaviours such as straying in search of the opposite sex and preventing unwanted pregnancies, there can also be health benefits. Neutering will eliminate the risk of pyometra (see page 121) in bitches and testicular cancer in male dogs, as well as reducing the likelihood of breast and prostate cancers.

Spaying is a fairly major operation for bitches, involving complete removal of the ovaries and uterus. Some vets like to carry it out at around 5 months, before the first season, but others feel that allowing a season makes it easier to judge the best time for the operation, when the uterus has a minimal blood supply and hormonal levels are low. A more mature dog will also cope better with anaesthesia.

Castration in males – the removal of both testicles – is a simpler operation. Although it can be done earlier, most vets advise waiting until 6–18 months old, depending on breed. See also page 9 for more information on neutering.

Parasites

FLEAS

An adult flea can lay up to 50 eggs a day and under optimum conditions the lifecycle can be completed within 15 days, so they can multiply rapidly, making your dog intensely itchy and miserable.

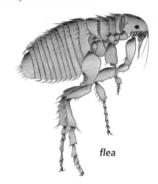

flea

Life cycle

- Adult fleas mate while on your dog and the eggs that are laid fall off as he wanders around. These eggs can be carried on your shoes and clothing into other people's homes.
- A couple of days later the eggs hatch into larvae which wriggle away from the light.
- After three moulting stages, the mature larvae spin themselves cocoons which protect them as they develop into adult fleas. They can survive up to two years in this state. Heat, motion, vibration and an increase in carbon dioxide levels (indicating the presence of a potential host) cause them to hatch out.
- The adult flea jumps on to its host and feeds by inserting long mouthparts into the skin, followed by an injection of saliva to prevent the blood from clotting. It is this saliva, rather than the bite itself, that causes irritation.

Diseases from fleas

Flea bites can trigger allergic reactions in some dogs, leading to inflamed itchy areas which can develop into large open sores. Fleas may also infect your pet with tapeworm (see page 113), and can transmit two bacteria known to cause mild flu-like symptoms, fever and a skin rash in humans.

Detecting fleas

Obvious signs of flea infestation include your dog frequently scratching, licking or chewing at himself, pink bite marks on his skin, or if you actually spot a flea. Check for fleas by gently brushing against the lie of the hair at the base of the tail. Catch any debris you flick out on a damp piece of white paper: flea dirt will dissolve to leave a reddish-brown stain.

Getting rid of fleas

Some anti-flea products are insecticidal, others act as repellents or have a contraceptive effect on fleas. They are available as collars, powders, shampoos, sprays, tablets and 'spot-on' treatments. Some are fast-acting, others may take several days, and effectiveness varies from 24 hours to 3 months. Consult your vet about suitability. You can also buy non-chemical products, including flea combs, flea traps and pest repellents.

Environmental management is also important. For every flea you spot on your dog there are another 99 lurking around your house in various stages of development. As well as chemical control, regular and thorough vacuuming is highly effective at eliminating all life stages of fleas.

TIP Treat all animals in your house at the same time, not just those showing signs of fleas.

TIP If your dog has fleas treat for tapeworm too.

Persistent scratching can be a sign of flea infestation or skin problems.

TICKS

Ticks can transmit infections such as Lyme disease, so use preventative products available from your vet if you will be walking your dog in an area known for them. If your dog does pick up a tick, do not attempt to burn it off or dab it with petroleum jelly, butter or alcohol, as this will stress the tick and cause it to empty its stomach contents into your dog's bloodstream.

1. Remove the tick with a tick-remover – available from pet shops or your vet.
2. Check that the mouthparts have not been left embedded in the skin, then dab the area with a mild antiseptic and wash your hands.
3. If you notice pain or swelling at the site, or if your dog appears lethargic, consult your vet.

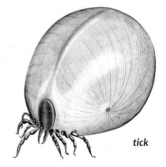

tick

Safety

Some active ingredients in canine anti-flea treatments can be lethal to cats and other companion animals, so care needs to be taken in selecting a product. Do not assume that herbal products or those based on essential oils are automatically safe because they are labelled 'natural'. Always read and follow the manufacturer's instructions.

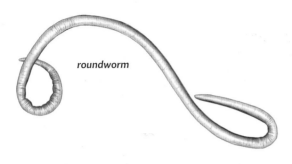

roundworm

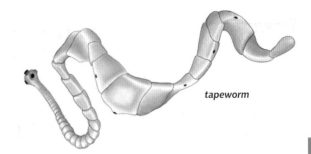

tapeworm

WORMS

All dogs will have worms at some point in their lives, although they may not show signs of it unless they are heavily infested.

Types of worms

In the UK there are two main types of worm affecting dogs:

Roundworms. The commonest is *Toxocara canis*, which can grow up to 18 cm long and looks like threads or strands of spaghetti, depending on size. They live on partially digested food in the bowel. Adults release as many as 100,000 microscopic eggs a day into the environment in the dog's faeces.

Tapeworms. The commonest is *Dipylidium caninum*, which can reach up to 70 cm in length. Made up of strings of long, flat segments, they use sharp teeth to attach themselves to the gut wall. New segments packed with eggs are continuously produced and gradually break off to be expelled with the dog's faeces. They look like tiny white rice grains and may wriggle for a short time before drying up. Sometimes they become stuck around the anus, causing irritation which the dog attempts to relieve by scooting his bottom along the ground – although more often

Bottom-dragging may be due to worms or painful anal glands.

this behaviour is due to blocked or infected anal glands which will need veterinary attention.

Less often seen are **whipworms**, **hookworms** and **lungworms**: these last, carried by slugs and snails, have been gradually increasing. If you plan to take your dog abroad, you should consult your vet about preventative medication for **heartworm**.

How can my dog get worms?

When your dog licks, sniffs and plays on contaminated areas he picks up roundworm eggs on his muzzle, paws and coat, which are then ingested when he licks or grooms himself. Eggs can remain infective in grass or soil for two or more years, so making sure you always clear up your dog's poop will help reduce the risk.

Tapeworms differ in that the eggs need to be eaten by an intermediate host. In the case of *Dipylidium caninum*, this is a flea: when your dog swallows an infected flea during grooming, the lifecycle continues.

Health risks

Worms can damage the dog's gut; cause diarrhoea, vomiting, anaemia, coughing and weight loss; stunt growth, cause blockages and in some cases can be fatal. They can also pose health risks to humans. If *Toxocara canis* eggs are ingested by humans they may develop into larvae which travel around the body to the lungs, liver and sometimes the eyes, where they can cause impaired or complete loss of vision. Hygiene precautions such as washing your hands after handling your dog and not sharing food with him are therefore important – particularly for children, who are especially vulnerable.

Treating your dog for worms

If you wait until symptoms of infection appear, infestation may be heavy and much damage done. Wormers will remove only worms already present and will leave the system after a few days. As they have no residual effect they will not protect against further re-infection, so you will need to worm on a regular basis. Puppies are especially vulnerable to roundworm and can be born already infected. Roundworm may also be passed on by the mother through her milk or when she licks her pups, so the youngsters should be wormed every 2–3 weeks until 12 weeks old, then monthly until 6 months old. From 6 months onwards, worm every 3 months. Dogs inclined to scavenge or who are heavily infested may need worming more frequently.

Which wormer should you choose?

Wormers are available in a number of different forms – tablets, pastes, granules, syrups, liquids, spot-ons and injections. Some are specific to particular types or life stages of worms, and some are not recommended for particular breeds of dog. Ask your vet for advice on a suitable worming programme when you first get your dog, and discuss it again during annual check-ups.

TIP Worm all animals in your household at the same time.

TIP If your dog has tapeworms treat for fleas too.

EMERGENCY FIRST AID

Your dog's health

First aid kit

You can buy a ready-made first aid kit from a pet shop or put one together yourself. Carry a small basic version with you when out on walks and keep a more comprehensive one at home and in the car.

- **Sterile saline sachets** – used for cleaning wounds.
- **Cotton wool** – never use dry: always soak in water, saline or antiseptic solution to clean wounds.
- **Alcohol-free wound-cleaning wipes** – useful for cleaning small grazes or cleaning your own hands.
- **Latex gloves** – put on before dealing with cuts and wounds to protect you and your dog from infection.
- **Sterile non-adherent wound dressings** – used to cover open wounds and prevent bandages from sticking to them. Usually placed with the shiny side on the wound. Try not to touch the sterile surface when opening the packet and putting the dressing in place.
- **Padded bandage** – used to hold dressings in place. Will absorb any excess blood and provides a comfortable padded layer.
- **Conforming bandage** – a mesh-like fabric used to keep padded bandages in place. Can be used to apply pressure on top of a padded bandage to stem heavy bleeding.
- **Adhesive tape** – secures bandages in place.
- **Cohesive bandage** – can be used as a top layer, keeping the padded- and conforming-bandage layers clean. It sticks to itself and conforms to the shape of what you're bandaging.
- **White open-weave bandage** – useful for an emergency muzzle or splint.
- **Tweezers** – for pulling out thorns, grass seeds, insect stings and splinters.
- **Tick-remover**.
- **Scissors** – for cutting bandages or trimming hair away from the edges of wounds.
- **Space blanket** – useful for keeping an injured dog warm.

Rules of first aid

- **Keep calm.**
- **Assess the situation.** Check whether it is safe to approach the dog and decide what needs to be done.
- **Protect yourself from bites.** Even the most sweet-natured dog may snap when in pain and frightened, so contain and restrain as needed.
- **Get veterinary help as soon as possible.** The Veterinary Surgeons Act 1966 allows you to administer emergency first aid to your dog. This means that until you can get professional help, your job is to do only what is necessary to preserve life, reduce pain and relieve suffering. It is the vet's job actually to diagnose and treat injuries.

TIP In an emergency ring the vet so they can be ready for your arrival. If you just turn up out of hours, there may be no one there.

Emergency A–Z

BITE INJURIES

If your dog has been involved in a fight with another animal, always take him to the vet as puncture wounds can often become infected and a course of antibiotics may be advisable. If he has been involved in a cat fight, the tips of claws may have broken off in his wounds, and his eyes should also be checked for scratches.

BURNS

Prevention is best. Don't allow your dog in the kitchen while you are cooking and keep him away from barbecues. Store chemicals out of reach, use fireguards in front of fires and unplug electrical appliances when your dog is left unattended.

Burn types and causes

Chemical. Domestic and other chemicals, such as paint-stripper, weedkiller, oven cleaner, bleach, battery acid, creosote.

Dry. Flames, contact with cooker hobs, cigarettes; also friction burns – e.g. from jumping out of a moving car.

Electrical. Most commonly from chewing through electrical cables.

Radiation. Sunburn – pink noses and hairless areas can be vulnerable in hot weather. Protect with sunblock.

Scalds. Steam, hot liquids, hot oil.

Open fires can be dangerous unless a fireguard is used.

Emergency action

1. Smother any flames with a jacket or blanket. For scald-type burns caused by hot oil or fat, remove as much of the liquid as possible with paper towel.
2. Immediate cooling of the area is vital. Ideally use a continuous stream of cool water from a spray, hosepipe or shower attachment; or you can use clean sheets, towels or gauze swabs soaked in water. Continue cooling for at least 10 minutes to stop burning and relieve pain.
3. Cover with a non-stick sterile dressing to keep the area clean and prevent infection, or cover with clingfilm and place a cold, wet teatowel over the top. Place another layer of dressing over that and lightly secure with a bandage while you transport your dog to the vet.

Chemical burns

Use rubber gloves to handle your dog so that you are not burned too. Use plenty of water to wash the affected area, trying to avoid flushing it over the rest of his body. Continue rinsing for at least 20 minutes. Do not allow him to lick his coat, as this may cause additional complications.

If the inside of his mouth is burned, lie him on his side and pour water through his mouth (but not down his throat).

Provide details of the chemical or product when you go to the vet.

Electrical burns

If your dog has suffered an electrical burn, switch off the electricity supply before touching him. Electrical shock may cause cardiac arrest, so check for breathing and heartbeat and if necessary give artificial respiration or CPR (see page 117). Even if your dog seems fine, still take him to the vet as the effects may appear later and be fatal.

DIARRHOEA

Diarrhoea can be linked to other problems, but is often due to eating inappropriate foods or a sudden change in diet. If you suspect this:

- Withhold food for 24 hours (puppies for 12 hours). Allow free access to water.
- Give small meals of easy-to-digest, bland food, such as two-thirds boiled white rice to one-third boiled chicken or white fish. When bowel movements are normal, slowly re-introduce the usual diet.

Consult your vet if:

- The problem persists for more than 48 hours after treatment starts.
- You notice the presence of any blood.
- Your dog is also vomiting, lethargic, in pain or has a temperature more than 1°C above normal.
- You think he may have eaten something harmful.

Keep rubbish bins out of reach.

HEATSTROKE

Short-nosed breeds, or dogs who are very young, old, overweight, have had previous episodes of heatstroke or suffer from heart or respiratory disorders are most at risk of overheating during hot weather. Exercise your dog in the early morning or late evening when it is cooler and never leave him in the car. Signs of heatstroke include:

- Initial restlessness, barking and whining.
- Excessive panting, becoming laboured, with copious drooling of saliva.
- Struggling to breathe. Gums may be dark red and eyes glassy.
- Seizures, coma.

Emergency action

1. Remove dog to a shady area and begin cooling as soon as the first signs are noticed. Use cool but not cold or icy water from a hosepipe, bath, shower or bucket of water and sponges. The most important areas to concentrate on are the inside of the upper thighs, armpits and base of the brain. If immersing his body in water, support his head above the surface.
2. Continue cooling for 10 minutes, after which take your dog to the vet, even though he may appear fully recovered.

HYPOTHERMIA

Cold conditions can be life-threatening, especially for very young and elderly dogs, or those with thin coats. Do not allow your dog to swim in rivers in cold weather: even when mild the water can be extremely cold and he can become chilled through. Do not let him walk on frozen water in case the ice gives way and he falls in. Wash and dry paws if snow gets trapped on hair between the toes as this can cause frostbite. Signs of hypothermia include:

- Shivering.
- Disorientation.
- Drowsiness.
- Exhaustion.
- Rectal temperature below 36.7°C.

Emergency action

1. Wrap dog warmly in blankets, covering body, legs and paws.
2. Place a hotwater or microwavable bottle against his belly – wrap it in a towel first.
3. Seek veterinary attention.

Cold weather can be as dangerous as hot.

INSECT STINGS

Stings are usually more painful than serious, but severe reactions can sometimes occur.

Emergency action

1. If the sting is still present, remove it with tweezers, taking care not to squeeze the venom sac.
2. Use a cold compress to soothe and reduce swelling.
3. If available, vinegar applied to wasp stings and a paste made of bicarbonate of soda and water to bee stings may help.
4. Stings in the mouth or throat may require rapid veterinary intervention if swelling interferes with breathing or if the dog has an allergic response. Signs of this include rapid swelling, difficulty in breathing, distress, weakness and collapse.

POISONING

For advice on poisonous plants and foodstuffs, see pages 49, 51 and 62. If you suspect that your dog has eaten something toxic, prompt action is essential. Signs of poisoning can be many and varied, including:

- Coughing, shortness of breath.
- Bleeding from mouth and anus, acute vomiting.
- Weakness, muscle tremors.
- Loss of coordination, seizures, collapse.

Emergency action

Call your vet immediately: provide as much information as possible about what you think your dog has eaten.

You may be told to make him vomit to reduce absorption of the substance. Do this by placing one or two washing (**not** caustic) soda crystals on the back of the tongue. Vomiting should follow shortly. Never induce vomiting if the substance swallowed is caustic or corrosive.

Transport your dog to the vet as quickly as possible. Take any packaging with you. Details of the substance or product are important as treatment needs to be specific to the toxin to give the best chance of success.

SHOCK

Shock can kill unless treated quickly. Common causes are heavy external or internal bleeding, dehydration (e.g. after severe diarrhoea or vomiting) and heart failure. Signs include:

- Rapid breathing and pulse, becoming shallow and irregular.
- Gums pale, becoming pale blue as shock develops.
- Cool ears and paws.
- Slow return of colour to gums after fingertip pressure is released (see page 109). As shock develops, this can slow to more than 4 seconds.
- Weak, lethargic, lapsing into unconsciousness.

Emergency action

If your dog is in, or going into, shock:
1. Keep him warm, quiet and still. Give nothing to eat or drink. If he is unconscious, raise his hindquarters so they are higher than his head.
2. Watch ABCs (see page 117).
3. Stop any obvious bleeding.
4. Seek urgent veterinary attention.

VOMITING

Dogs often vomit to rid themselves of unwanted food or foreign objects in their stomachs. It may also be due to motion sickness (see page 107). There is usually just a single episode. If your dog seems otherwise healthy, withhold food and water for a few hours, by which time he should have returned to normal. However, consult your vet the same day if vomiting is:

- Persistent.
- Violent or projectile.
- Bloody.
- Accompanied by pain, lethargy, fever, diarrhoea or any other symptoms that give concern.

WOUNDS

Minor wounds that haven't broken all the way through the skin don't usually need veterinary attention. Clean them thoroughly with saline solution.

Wounds needing stitches

A cut which has gone through the full skin layer may bleed quite profusely and is likely to need stitching.

Emergency action

Flush with saline solution to clean. Do not use wound cream or powders.

Bandage (see page 114) and take to the vet. The sooner the wound is stitched, the more likely it is to heal quickly and cleanly.

Heavy bleeding

If a vein or artery is damaged there may be a considerable amount of blood. Venous blood is dark and oozes, while arterial blood is bright red and may spurt rhythmically.

Emergency action

Cover with a sterile pad, then with a large absorbent pad such as a piece of cotton wool. Bandage this layer firmly in place. If blood seeps through, apply more padding and bandage over the top, adding further layers as needed.

Keep the injured area elevated if possible to lessen blood flow. Watch for shock. Get to a vet as quickly as possible. Try not to move him more than necessary as this will make the heart beat harder, increasing blood loss; carry rather than walk him.

Cleaning wounds

- Don't scrub or poke at a wound when cleaning it, as this is likely to push dirt in more deeply.
- Never use dry cotton wool as the fibres will stick to the injury. Always soak swabs and change them frequently so that you don't keep reintroducing dirt.
- You can also use a plastic syringe (minus needle) to run saline solution over the injury without touching it directly if the area is very tender.
- You can make your own saline solution: dissolve one teaspoonful of salt in one pint of water.

Dressings

Once treated, wounds are usually best left exposed to the air, though it may be necessary to put a dressing on for protection or to keep the site clean. This will need to be kept clean and dry, as a wet bandage can shrink and restrict circulation. Protect it with a plastic bag and tape or cohesive bandage when your dog goes outside.

RESUSCITATION

If your dog's breathing or heartbeat stops after an injury, it is essential to get veterinary assistance as soon as possible. In the meantime you can attempt to resuscitate him as follows.

Assess your dog's condition

If your dog's breathing stops, you can supply oxygen to the lungs by giving him artificial respiration. Should his heart stop beating, heart massage may re-start it. If both breathing and heartbeat stop, the two techniques can be used together and are known as 'cardiopulmonary resuscitation' or CPR. This is most likely to be needed in situations such as choking, drowning, electrocution and shock. Artificial respiration should be given only if the dog is not breathing and heart massage only if the heartbeat has ceased.

- Check it is safe to approach the dog and that there are no other hazards to attend to first.
- Check the dog's level of consciousness by calling his name, tapping him and pinching between his toes. If there is little or no response, follow the same 'ABC' as for humans – Airway, Breathing, Circulation:

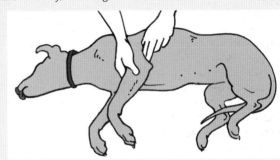

Airway. Lie the dog on his right-hand side, if possible with his head slightly lower than the rest of his body. Stretch his head and neck out to straighten the airway. Check whether an object or debris inside the mouth is blocking the airway, remove if there is, then draw the tongue forwards slightly.

Breathing. Check for breathing by looking along the dog's ribcage to see if the chest is rising and falling, and listen for the sound of breathing. If it is very faint use a strand of hair to check (see page 109).

Circulation. Use your hand to feel for a heartbeat or pulse (see page 109).

Artificial respiration

Briskly rub the dog's sides for 30 seconds to stimulate breathing. If this fails, start artificial respiration. Make sure the airway is still open, pull the tongue forwards slightly and place one or both hands round the muzzle to hold the mouth closed. Place your own mouth around the dog's nose to form a seal and blow just hard enough to make the chest rise.

Remove your mouth and allow his lungs to deflate. Repeat. Give one breath every 3–5 seconds. Remove your mouth after each breath to allow the lungs to deflate again.

If the dog starts breathing again, stop giving artificial respiration, otherwise continue. After every four or five breaths, check if the pulse or heartbeat is still present. If the heart stops, begin heart massage.

Heart massage

Position the heel of one hand on the ribcage where the elbow touches the body. Place your other hand on top and press quickly and firmly downwards and towards the neck. Repeat at a rate of 60–100 times a minute.

If the dog is very small (see inset drawing), grasp the chest between the thumb and forefingers of one hand just behind his elbows and squeeze together to compress the ribcage while you support his body with your other hand.

After every five compressions give another breath (after every three compressions for very small dogs).

If the heart starts again, stop heart massage but continue with artificial respiration if necessary.

Continue until veterinary help can be obtained.

CARING FOR A CONVALESCENT DOG

Following surgery, you may need to take special care of your dog. Good nursing will contribute to a successful outcome.

Recovery after surgery

When you collect your dog he may still be woozy from the anaesthetic, with poor balance and coordination. Lift him in and out of the car, keep him warm and drive carefully on the way home. Once home:

Take your dog outside to relieve himself. He'll probably then want to sleep, and may be drowsy for up to 24–36 hours.

Check the operation site daily. There is no need to bathe it unless instructed to do so. Use an Elizabethan collar if necessary to stop him from worrying at it. If the wound is bandaged, watch out for swelling above or below the dressing, and for seeping fluids.

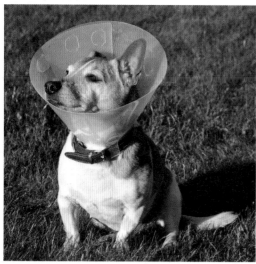

A special collar will prevent your dog licking at wounds.

Exercise may be restricted for a certain period. Keep him on a leash when you take him out, and discourage running up and down stairs or jumping on to furniture. If he lacks mobility, bring water to him frequently.

Make arrangements for any physiotherapy recommended, such as hydrotherapy. Check your insurance policy, as this may be covered.

TIP Always finish a course of medication, even if your pet is looking better. This is especially important with antibiotics.

TIP If medications are vomited up, do not give more without consulting the vet first.

Giving medication

Always give medication at the intervals recommended.
Tablets. Disguise inside a piece of sausage or cheese. Alternatively, crush and sprinkle on food, or mix with peanut butter or cream cheese and smear on your dog's tongue.

If pills must be given whole, cannot be given with food, or if your dog refuses to take them no matter how well disguised, you will need to give them in the following way:

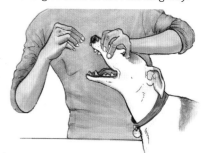

1. Place one hand over the top of his muzzle, fingers on one side and thumb on the other just behind the canine teeth.
2. Tilt his head upwards and, with the tablet ready in your other hand, use one or two fingers to draw the lower jaw downwards.
3. Drop the tablet as far back in his mouth as possible. Keep his head tilted upwards, hold his jaws closed with one hand and massage his throat with the other until he swallows. Praise him.

Liquid medicines. Keeping your dog's head level, squirt the medicine gently into the side of his mouth. Hold his jaws closed, rub his throat until he swallows and then praise him.

Ear drops. Hold the nozzle of the ear-drop applicator over the opening of the ear canal and squeeze out the prescribed number of drops. Gently massage around the base of the ear to spread the medication around, and praise him.

Eye drops/ointment. Tilt your dog's head slightly upwards. Squeeze a drop directly on to his eye. If using ointment, warm the tube in your hands first so that it flows more easily. Draw a lower lid down to form a pocket and squeeze a line of ointment into it: gently release the lid and praise.

Signs for concern

Contact your vet if you have concerns or if you notice:
- Deepening unconsciousness.
- Paws feeling cold or clammy and gums pale.
- Full consciousness or full control of limbs not regained after 36 hours.
- Allergic reactions or swelling of mouth, face or throat.
- Persistent retching or vomiting.
- Faeces containing blood.
- Bleeding, acute swelling, redness, oozing or unpleasant smell at the operation site.
- Worrying at, or pulling out, stitches.

DISEASE A–Z

The following guide provides a brief explanation of ailments mentioned elsewhere in this book. It is not a guide to diagnosis or treatment, both of which should be left to a veterinary practitioner. If you have **any** concerns about your dog's health, you should **always** consult a vet. Cross-references to other entries in the A–Z appear in *italics*.

Arthritis
Inflammation of a joint, causing mild to severe pain. Symptoms may include stiffness, *lameness*, reduced range of movement, reluctance to play, exercise, walk on slippery surfaces or stairs. See also page 124.

Bad breath
Although most commonly due to dental disease (see page 67), bad breath can also be an indication of other health problems, including *diabetes*, *kidney disease*, lung conditions and digestive disorders.

Bloat
This condition occurs when the stomach flips over, interfering with blood supply and preventing food and gas from entering or leaving. Large, deep-chested dogs are most at risk. Immediate veterinary attention is essential, but even then it can prove fatal. See also page 64.

Blood disorders
These include auto-immune haemolytic anaemia (AIHA), in which red blood cells are destroyed by the immune system more quickly than new ones can be produced, and haemophilia, a clotting disorder. Disorders may be mild or severe in effect and sudden or slow in onset. Symptoms can include poor appetite, weakness, pale or yellowish gums, nosebleeds and prolonged bleeding following injury or surgery.

Bottom-dragging
The most usual cause is blocked anal glands, which can usually be emptied quite easily by a vet, though severe cases may require surgery. Can also be caused by worms (see page 113).

Cancer
Dogs can be affected by a number of different cancers and particular breeds have an increased tendency towards certain types. Some cancers can be successfully treated these days. See also page 124.

Canine distemper
Also known as hardpad, this disease affects the nervous system and can be fatal. Symptoms include loss of appetite, *vomiting*, *diarrhoea*, lethargy, discharge from eyes and nose. See also 'Vaccination', page 111.

Canine infectious hepatitis
Highly contagious, this disease affects the liver and can be fatal in puppies. Dogs who recover may infect others for months after and may suffer kidney damage. Symptoms include loss of appetite, abdominal pain, raised temperature, loss of coordination, *vomiting* and *diarrhoea* (with blood seen in later stages), pale gums, seizures. See also 'Vaccination', page 111.

Canine parvovirus
Highly contagious virus spread through contaminated faeces and affecting the intestines and bowel. Symptoms include raised temperature, coughing, abdominal pain, bloody *diarrhoea* and *vomiting*. Can be fatal. See also 'Vaccination', page 111.

Cataracts
Hardening of the lens of the eye causes it to become cloudy, interfering with vision. This may be due to old age, but may also occur as a result of *diabetes*. Hereditary in some breeds.

'Cherry eye'
Swelling of the gland behind the third eyelid (see page 39) causes it to protrude from the corner of the eye. Surgery is required.

Collie eye anomaly
Inherited condition in which a problem with blood supply results in a detached retina, causing blindness in the affected eye. There is no treatment.

Constipation
Straining or inability to pass faeces can be due to a number of factors, including insufficient water intake, enlarged prostate, or a blockage caused by something eaten or by a tumour. See also page 124.

Copper toxicosis
An inherited condition in which inefficient excretion of copper from the body leads to a progressive build-up in the liver, which then becomes damaged.

Coughing
May be a symptom of many problems, ranging from an object stuck in the throat to *kennel cough*, *heart problems*, heartworm (see page 113) and tumours.

Cryptorchidism
One or both testicles fail to descend into the scrotum, increasing the risk of testicular *cancer* unless surgically removed.

Cushing's disease
Overactive adrenal glands cause a number of symptoms including increased appetite, drinking and urination; also hair loss, thinning skin, muscle-wasting, panting, skin infections and slow, poor wound-healing.

Deafness
Loss of hearing may be due to old age, blockage of the ear canals by wax or ear infections, but in some breeds may be inherited. Can occur in one or both ears. See also pages 67 and 124.

Diabetes
Lack of insulin production or inability to utilize it causes raised blood sugar. If left untreated can be life-threatening. Symptoms include increased appetite, thirst and urination, weight loss and lethargy. May cause *cataracts* and urinary tract infections.

Diarrhoea
Often due to a stomach upset, but can lead to dehydration (see page 63) and may also be a symptom of a number of diseases. Persistent or bloody diarrhoea should be a cause for concern. See also page 115.

Drooling
Although it is normal for some breeds to produce large amounts of saliva, excessive drooling can indicate a mouth problem, *bloat*, heatstroke (see page 115), poisoning (see page 116) and other conditions, as well as being a response to fear.

'Dry eye'
Hereditary in some breeds, Tear production is insufficient to lubricate the eyes, leading to ulceration and infection.

Ectropion
Sagging and rolling outwards of the lower eyelid leads to inflammation. More common in breeds with loose facial skin. May require surgical correction if severe.

Elbow dysplasia
Abnormal development of the elbow joint, causing pain and lameness in the affected foreleg and likely to require surgery.

Entropion

Inward turning of the eyelids, causing irritation and ulceration. If severe, may need surgical correction. May be an inherited condition in some breeds.

Epilepsy

Disturbance in the electrical activity of the brain causing seizures which may involve loss of consciousness accompanied by involuntary movement, salivation, urination, defecation. Partial seizures are more subtle, with the dog remaining conscious. Epilepsy can be an inherited disorder but seizures may also occur due to causes such as exposure to toxins, head injury, low blood sugar, brain tumour, heatstroke (see page 115).

Eye disorders

Breeds with prominent eyes may be more prone to injury than others. There are also a number of eye diseases that may affect dogs: see 'Cherry eye', Collie eye anomaly, 'Dry eye', Ectropion, Entropion, Glaucoma and Progressive retinal atrophy (PRA).

Foot problems

See Lameness.

Fucosidosis

A fatal inherited condition caused by an enzyme deficiency, affecting the nervous system of Springer Spaniels. Symptoms include behavioural changes, seizures, and loss of balance, coordination, hearing and vision.

Glaucoma

Very painful condition caused by increased pressure within the eye, which may look cloudy, bloodshot, produce continual tears and appear to bulge. Early treatment is essential if sight is to be saved.

Heart problems

Heart muscles, valves or the main blood vessels to or from the heart may be affected, causing symptoms including panting, coughing, weakness, loss of appetite and weight, depression, abnormal heart rhythms, fainting, blueness of the gums. See also page 124.

Hip dysplasia

A painful defect of the hip joints where a loose fit of the ball-and-socket joint leads to the head of the femur rubbing on the edges of the socket and causing arthritic changes. Symptoms include pain, difficulty in getting up and in going upstairs. Weight control, careful exercise, pain management and dietary supplements are likely to be prescribed. In severe cases surgery may be required.

Hypothyroidism

Underactive thyroid gland. Symptoms include lethargy, hair loss, slow heart rate, constipation, weight gain, dull dry coat. Affected dogs will also be more susceptible to infections and less tolerant of cold.

Incontinence

Uncontrolled dribbling of urine, which may be due to senility/old age (see pages 123 and 124) or to urinary infections or prostate problems. Can sometimes occur in females after spaying (see page 111).

Inherited diseases

Over 400 inherited diseases have now been identified in dogs and it is important to be aware of any health problems associated with your choice of breed. Tests are available for many hereditary diseases, so buy from a reputable breeder who uses these schemes. The relevant breed club will be able to provide you with information on any health issues and screening tests. See also 'Potential health problems' chart, page 18.

Kennel cough

Highly contagious disease of the respiratory system, caused by a variety of viruses and bacteria. Symptoms include dry cough, lethargy, raised temperature, lack of appetite, eye and nasal discharge. Rarely fatal, although severe cases in puppies, older dogs and giant breeds can lead to pneumonia.

Kidney diseases

Causes include leptospirosis, urinary tract infection, blood poisoning, heatstroke (see page 115), heart conditions, tumours. Symptoms include vomiting, blood in the urine, drinking and urinating more or not passing urine, lack of appetite, weight loss, lethargy, pale gums and bad breath. See also page 124.

Lameness

Can be due to a number of problems, including arthritis, fractures, sprains, and strains, but first check for the obvious: cuts in the feet, grass seeds working their way up under the skin between the toes, and broken nails.

Legg-Calve Perthes disease

Disease of the hip joint in which reduced blood supply to the top part of the thigh bone leads to the bone dying, causing pain and lameness. Surgery will be required.

Leptospirosis

Bacterial infection spread in the urine of carrier animals such as rats, affecting the liver and kidneys. Some dogs can become carriers, spreading the disease to others without showing symptoms themselves.

When they do occur, symptoms include lethargy, raised temperature, vomiting, increased thirst, bloody diarrhoea, and inflamed membranes which in severe cases may be jaundiced. Can be fatal.

Liver disease

Various diseases can affect the liver, including canine infectious hepatitis and leptospirosis. Symptoms include loss of appetite, vomiting, weight loss, depression, lethargy, yellow-tinged eye membranes and gums, increased drinking and urination, abdominal pain, raised temperature, seizures.

Narcolepsy

Neurological disorder characterized by the dog suddenly falling asleep. Episodes can occur even during periods of activity.

Neurological problems

Problems which affect the nervous system, including canine distemper, deafness, epilepsy, narcolepsy, rabies, slipped disc and Wobbler syndrome.

Osteochondritis dissecans

Fragment of cartilage peeling away from the bone within a joint leads to inflammation and arthritic changes. Joints most frequently affected are the shoulder, elbow, stifle and hock. May be hereditary in some breeds, and is also associated with rapid growth rates. Symptoms include pain and lameness which improves with rest and worsens with exercise. Surgery may be required.

Panosteitis

Inflammation of the humerus, ulna and radius of the front legs, and femur and tibia of the back legs, which affects young, growing dogs. Pain may be mild or severe with lameness, loss of appetite and weight and a raised temperature. Painkillers and rest may be prescribed. The problem passes in most dogs as they mature.

Panting

A dog will pant when it is hot and after strenuous exercise, if in pain or stressed. It can also be a sign of heatstroke (see page 115), heart problems, respiratory problems, and numerous other ailments.

Parainfluenza

Virus produces symptoms which include coughing, retching, loss of appetite, watery eyes, nasal discharge. Can be a cause of kennel cough. Unpleasant but rarely fatal.

Patellar luxation

Kneecaps which slide out of place. The affected joint may lock and will not bear weight. In mild cases it may pop back into position again by itself. May require surgical correction.

Progressive retinal atrophy (PRA)

Hereditary eye condition in which blood supply to the retina decreases, causing it to deteriorate. Eventually leads to blindness.

Pyometra

Bacterial infection of the uterus, which fills with pus. Symptoms include excessive thirst, abnormal discharge from the vulva, dullness, *vomiting*. This is a veterinary emergency. Can be fatal.

Rabies

A virus transmitted through contaminated saliva and affecting the nervous system. Symptoms include drooling, aggression, sensitivity to light, and paralysis. Usually fatal.

Respiratory problems

Short-nosed breeds can have problems caused by small nostrils and elongated soft palates, causing snuffling, snorting, snoring and in severe cases fainting. Surgery may be necessary. Respiratory problems may also be due to conditions including heart problems, heatstroke (see page 115) and *kennel cough*.

Skin disorders

Dogs may be prone to a range of problems, including allergies triggered by food or contact with irritants such as flea bites (see page 112), yeast infections, mites, acne, seborrhoea (an increased activity of the skin's oil-producing glands) and ringworm. Symptoms include hair loss, rashes and inflamed patches of skin. The dog may lick, bite, chew or scratch at affected areas. Breeds with lots of folds in the skin or jowls may be more susceptible to infections.

Spinal problems

Problems include *Wobbler syndrome* and chronic degenerative radiculomyopathy (CDRM), a condition in which loss of hind-leg coordination progresses to partial paralysis. Slipped discs are common in short-legged, long-backed breeds. Symptoms include sudden pain, *lameness*, hunched posture, partial or complete paralysis.

Vomiting

Often due to a digestive upset, but can also be a symptom of more serious ailments, including *canine distemper, canine parvovirus, leptospirosis*, liver or kidney failure, an object blocking part of the gut, poisoning (see page 116), *pyometra* or worms (see page 113). See also page 116.

Wobbler syndrome

Pressure on the spinal cord in the neck region causing weakness and loss of coordination in all four legs. Severe cases may require surgery.

Zoonoses

Diseases which are transmissible between dogs and humans include *leptospirosis, rabies*, roundworm and tapeworm (see page 113), and some skin conditions including ringworm and scabies. Dogs can also sometimes be carriers of the gastrointestinal bacteria campylobacter and salmonella, as well as disease-carrying ticks (see page 112). Owners should be aware of such risks, but provided regular vaccinations, worming (see pages 111 and 113) and hygiene precautions such as poop-scooping and hand-washing are observed, any threat is relatively small.

Insurance

Veterinary fees can be very expensive should your dog become ill or injured. Taking out an insurance policy will help ensure you can pay for treatment if it is needed. Before you take out insurance, it is important to read carefully through the full policy of terms, and query anything that isn't clear.

POINTS TO CONSIDER

Claims. Is there a limit to the number of claims you can make each year? Check also the procedure for making a claim: will the insurance provider accept claims directly from the vet or will you have to pay the bill and wait for the company to reimburse you?

Age. Will cover cease at a certain age, be limited to accident-only, or have higher premiums and excesses applied?

Levels of cover. The cheapest is usually confined to a fixed limit within a certain period of time. This means your cover could expire while still in mid-treatment and you would then have to meet further costs yourself. Next cheapest is cover which will pay out for a condition each year it continues, up to a fixed limit – once that limit is reached you then have to pay for any further veterinary costs. Most expensive is 'cover for life', paying for treatment up to a fixed amount every year for as long as your dog needs treatment, with the 'limit' being renewed annually. This is useful in the event of long-term illnesses requiring ongoing treatment such as epilepsy, diabetes and arthritis.

Excess. Is the amount you have to contribute when making a claim a fixed sum or a percentage of the full claim?

Breed and location. Some companies may charge a higher premium if you live in a certain area or own a particular breed of dog.

What's covered. Check whether home visits, overnight and emergency care are included, also any necessary physiotherapy or 'alternative' therapies. Look also for other applicable cover – for example, are you covered if holidaying abroad with your dog?

PROPOSAL FORMS

Be honest when filling in proposal forms: if you have been economical with the truth it will be found out if you need to make a claim, and you could find your policy worthless as a result. If you aren't sure what things you need to disclose, contact the insurance company.

THIRD PARTY PUBLIC LIABILITY

If you buy no other type of insurance you should at least ensure you have Third Party Public Liability cover. Should you be proven legally liable for the injury, illness or death of a third party as a result of an incident in which your dog is involved, you could face the prospect of paying out thousands of pounds – possibly much more – in compensation and legal costs.

Chapter 8

CARING FOR AN ELDERLY DOG

Many dogs remain bright, mentally alert, physically active and relatively healthy until well advanced in years. Even so, the effects of ageing will eventually and inevitably make themselves felt and it is therefore important to be on the alert for signs of age-related health and behavioural problems. Although there is no cure for ageing, there is a lot you can do either to treat or to delay the progression of many conditions, ensuring that your elderly friend enjoys a comfortable old age.

The decisions you make for your pet at the end of his life are just as important as those you make during it. It helps to know a little about your options so that you can be as well prepared as possible.

AGEING

As your dog reaches senior-citizen status he will begin to lose the coordination, balance, strength and ease of movement he enjoyed in his youth, and you will need to adapt to his new requirements.

Signs of ageing

As he grows older, you will begin to notice changes in his appearance and behaviour:

- Grey hairs around the muzzle.
- Skin and coat may become drier and smellier.
- More sedate when out on walks and less inclined to play or interact with you.
- Stiffer, less flexible joints.
- Not always hearing when you call.
- Deteriorating eyesight.
- Increase or decrease in weight.
- Teeth showing signs of wear and tear.
- Sleeping longer, and often more deeply.
- Incontinence.

Senility

As well as physical changes, you may notice behavioural ones. Elderly dogs sometimes become affected by Canine Cognitive Dysfunction (CCD), a condition similar to Alzheimer's disease in humans. Physical and chemical changes occur in the brain, affecting its function and leading to behaviours that can be very distressing for both dog and owner. Signs that your dog may be suffering from CCD include:

- Becoming disorientated – wandering aimlessly, losing his bearings, staring into space or at walls, getting stuck in corners or behind furniture.
- Reduced interaction – less enthusiastic about visitors arriving, no longer greeting you when you've been out, lack of interest in being petted or receiving attention.
- Disrupted sleep patterns – sleeping more during the day and less at night, restless and anxious, barking and whining for no apparent reason.
- Loss of house-training.

Similar symptoms can be caused by other health problems, so consult your vet to ensure a correct diagnosis. Nothing can be done to cure CCD, but medications, supplements and special diets available from your vet may be able to help counter the effects.

Making life comfortable

There are many ways in which, with a little thought and effort, you can ensure that your dog feels comfortable during his senior years:

Weight. Try to avoid letting him become overweight, as this will put increased strain on heart and lungs, as well as on joints, which may be stiff and arthritic.

Callouses. Keep an eye out for these on elbows and other bony prominences. If they look sore or cracked, consult your vet – it could lead to infections as well as discomfort.

Bedding. Make sure it is positioned out of draughts and is easy for him to get into and out of. Soft bedding will help reduce pressure points at vulnerable areas.

Collar. Choose a light, soft one.

Flooring. Place rugs or runners on slippery flooring so that weak and aching limbs aren't strained through trying to keep their footing.

Exercise. Important for mental stimulation as well as maintaining joint mobility, but tailor activity to your dog's ability. Several short walks a day will be better for him than one long one – and remember that in their desire to please some will do more than is comfortable for them, so tone down games too.

Grooming. Be gentle, but don't neglect coat and skin care, as it has a 'feel-good' as well as a practical value. It's easy to spend less time interacting with your dog as he grows older, so this is also a good way of giving him your undivided attention and affection.

Eating. Provide a raised food bowl so there will be less strain on his back and on his front legs.

Common age-related health problems

Arthritis

One of the commonest health conditions in senior dogs, this can be tremendously painful, seriously affecting quality of life. With age, general wear and tear can lead to the joints developing some degree of arthritic change. Symptoms can often be overlooked until they have progressed to the point where the dog is in severe pain. Tell-tale signs include clumsiness, lack of enthusiasm for playing, general stiffness (often more noticeable after exercise), reluctance to go up or down steps or jump into or out of the car, difficulty getting up from a lying position, lameness and yelping when touched. Consult your vet about the most appropriate treatment: there are highly effective drugs that can relieve your dog's discomfort. Your vet will advise on diet and exercise, which also play a role in managing arthritis.

Cancer

The older a dog becomes, the more likely he is to develop cancer. Many cancers, however, can be very successfully treated these days. Be especially vigilant if you own a breed prone to particular cancers (see page 18). Watch out for abnormal swellings, sores that don't heal, weight loss, changes in appetite, bleeding or discharges and difficulty in eating, swallowing, breathing, urinating or defecating.

Watch for the onset of age-related health problems.

Constipation

Older dogs may become constipated due to lack of muscle tone, diet, reduced exercise and insufficient water intake. If your dog is having problems, don't let him strain. Although increasing the fibre or water content of his food may be all that's needed, there could be a more serious problem, such as a growth, so consult your vet.

Deafness

If your elderly dog fails to respond to your verbal commands, he isn't necessarily ignoring you: he may be losing his hearing. Take him to the vet for a check-up in case the problem is due to an ear infection. If he is becoming deaf due to age, always approach him from the front so that he can see you coming and isn't startled, which might cause a defensive reaction. If you need to wake him, do so by placing a strong-smelling treat by his nose, or by tapping or scratching the side of the bed rather than touching him. Keep him on the leash when out on walks, as he won't hear your recall commands.

Heart disease

This can lead to noticeable symptoms, such as excessive panting, coughing, reduced ability to exercise, weight loss, build-up of fluid in the abdomen, and in extreme cases the dog may faint or collapse. Treatments may be available: consult your vet, with whom you will also need to discuss diet, weight and exercise.

Incontinence

Your old dog may become less able to control his bladder, so if an accident happens in the house don't scold – it's not his fault. There may be many causes, including urinary infections, senility, loss of sphincter control in bitches, prostate problems in males, or ageing of the nerves that supply the bladder and urethra. Accidents may also happen because an arthritic dog can't make it to the garden in time; because he is so deeply asleep he's unaware of the need to go; or because a condition such as diabetes or kidney disease makes him drink more and consequently he requires more frequent trips outdoors. There may be a treatable physical cause, so seek advice from your vet.

Kidney disease

The chance of kidney failure increases with age. Symptoms include increased thirst and urination, weight loss, lack of appetite, vomiting, diarrhoea and weakness, and bad breath. By the time signs appear the condition is usually fairly advanced, but a carefully balanced diet may help alleviate some of the symptoms and slow the progress of the condition. Your vet will advise.

Obesity

Older dogs often become overweight as they slow down and take less exercise. See page 111 for more information.

Vision

Cataracts are the most common eye problem in older dogs, causing a bluish-white clouding of the lens which eventually leads to blindness. Normal ageing of the lens can also lead to cloudy changes resembling cataracts, but these don't normally interfere with vision other than causing short-sightedness. A dog with, or developing, a vision problem may appear clumsy, bumping into objects or becoming more clingy when out on walks. Most dogs adapt well to loss of sight, but avoid moving furniture, pad any sharp projecting edges and remove any potential hazards in the garden.

Saying Goodbye

It may be uncomfortable for you to think about what will happen at the end of your dog's life, but it is a matter to which you should give some consideration before it becomes an immediate prospect.

The right decision

It is unusual for pets simply to die of old age, and if yours is in pain and unable to enjoy life any more, then allowing him to go peacefully and painlessly is the last great gift you can give him.

Having decided that euthanasia is the kindest option for your dog, decide which environment – at home or at the vet's surgery – will enable the procedure to be carried out with the minimum of distress for both of you. If you wish for a home visit, check that your vet provides this service. If you take your dog to the surgery instead, try to arrange to have the last appointment of the day so that there's no rush and you have time to spend with your dog both beforehand and afterwards.

What Will Happen?

Before the procedure, you will be asked to sign a consent form. If the dog is likely to be distressed or difficult, a sedative may be administered to keep him calm. Euthanasia is carried out by injecting an overdose of anaesthetic, causing him to slip rapidly into a deep and irreversible sleep. Breathing and heartbeat will stop very soon after. Sometimes the limbs will twitch, urine will be passed or a noise made, but this is not due to any pain. The vet will then check that there is no pulse or heartbeat and will tap the cornea of the eye to check there is no reflexive response.

Should You Be Present?

If you stay with your dog, try to remain calm until he has gone: there will be plenty of time for tears later. A nurse will generally be present to assist, but don't feel you have to let her take over from you unless that's what you want. Speak to your dog in a quiet voice and stroke him gently: he doesn't know what is going to happen and will have no fear of it. Concentrate your thoughts on these last moments together, showing him how much you love and care for him so that he slips away gently and without distress.

While it may be comforting for your dog to have someone familiar present, don't feel guilty if you just can't face it. If you are very distressed, he may sense your feelings and become anxious himself. You'll still be with him in spirit if not in physical contact – but you may find it helpful to see his body afterwards so that you can be assured that he is at peace and to say a final goodbye.

After death

Most people choose either burial or cremation. Your vet can help you organize your choices or you can arrange it yourself.

Burial

If burying your pet at home, make sure you dig a grave at least 1 metre deep. Put a paving slab or other heavy object on top to deter scavengers. Bear in mind that if you move house you will no longer be able to visit his last resting place.

If you prefer, you can have your dog buried in a pet cemetery; see your local Yellow Pages or ask your vet to recommend one. Pet cemeteries usually offer the options of individual or communal burial.

Cremation

Cremation can be done only at a special pet crematorium – see Yellow Pages or ask your vet for details. As with burial, you'll have the choice of individual or communal cremation. You can ask for your dog's ashes to be returned to you, or some crematoria can arrange for them to be scattered in a special pet garden of remembrance.

Coping with loss

The loss of a much-loved pet can be just as traumatic as that of a friend or relative. How long it takes to grieve varies from weeks to months or even years. Unfortunately, not everyone may understand the depth of your grief and it may help to talk to a sympathetic listener. Ask your doctor about counselling or, if you prefer, contact the Blue Cross Pet Bereavement Helpline – see page 126 for details.

If you have children, be honest when explaining what happened, as euphemisms may be misunderstood. Holding a short memorial service or making up a special scrapbook may help them, as well as you, to come to terms with your loss.

USEFUL CONTACTS

Agility Club
Details of local clubs, events and results.
Web www.agilityclub.co.uk

AllergyUK
Charity offering advice to sufferers.
Tel. 01322 619898
Email info@allergyuk.org
Web www.allergyuk.org

Animal Health Trust
Vetinerary charity dedicated to improving the health and welfare of dogs, cats and horses.
Tel. 01638 751000
Web www.aht.org.uk

Association of Dogs and Cats Homes
Contact details of shelters subscribing to ADCH-recommended standards.
Web www.adch.org.uk

Association of Pet Behaviour Counsellors
International network of counsellors who also offer advice on welfare.
Tel. 01386 751151
Email info@apbc.org.uk
Web www.apbc.org.uk

Association of Pet Dog Trainers (UK)
Promotes fair and humane training methods. Details of member trainers.
Tel. 01285 810811
Web www.apdt.co.uk

Association of Private Pet Cemeteries and Crematoria
Promotes a code of practice for members.
Tel. 01252 844478
Email contact@appcc.org.uk
Web www.appcc.org.uk

Battersea Dogs & Cats Home
London-based charity. Rehomes and provides a lost and found service. Also runs a pet behaviour advice line.
Tel. 020 7622 3626
Web www.battersea.org.uk
Lost Dogs & Cats Line 0901 477 8477
Behaviour Advice Line 0905 020 0222

Blue Cross
Charity aimed at all pets and horses. Rehomes animals and provides bereavement support.
Tel. 01993 822651
Email info@bluecross.org.uk
Web www.bluecross.org.uk

Blue Cross Pet Bereavement Support
Tel. 0800 096 6606
Email pbssmail@bluecross.org.uk

British Association of Homeopathic Veterinary Surgeons
UK professional body for homeopathic vets. Details available of practitioners.
Tel. 07708 322073
Web www.bahvs.com

British Flyball Association
UK governing body of international Flyball Racing: information, results and clubs.
Web www.flyball.org.uk

Department for Environment, Food and Rural Affairs (Defra)
Government department offering information on animal welfare laws and the rules for transportation of animals.
Tel. 08459 33 55 77
Email helpline@defra.gsi.gov.uk
Web www.defra.gov.uk

Dogs Trust
UK's largest dog welfare charity. Rehoming, outreach programmes, education, information, legislation and campaigning.
Tel. 020 7837 0006
Web www.dogstrust.org.uk

Dog Theft Action
Advice on prevention and action in the event of theft plus links to lost/stolen organizations.
Web www.dogtheftaction.com

Gundog Club
Information and details of tests, award schemes and training courses.
Web www.thegundogclub.co.uk

Kennel Club (UK)
UK charity which aims to promote the general improvement of dogs: welfare, health, training and breeding. Most countries have their own national Kennel Clubs with similar goals.
Tel. 0870 606 6750
Web www.thekennelclub.org.uk

PDSA
UK's leading veterinary charity. Provides free veterinary treatment and promotes responsible pet ownership.
Tel: 01952 290999
Web www.pdsa.org.uk

Pets as Therapy
Charity which provides therapeutic visits to hospices, hospitals, nursing and care homes and special needs schools by volunteers and assessed pets.
Tel. 01844 345445
Web www.petsastherapy.org

Royal College of Veterinary Surgeons
UK regulatory body for vets.
Tel. 020 7222 2001
Web www.rcvs.org.uk

Sound Therapy 4 Pets Ltd
Products and information on helping noise-sensitive pets overcome their fears.
Tel. 01244 371473
Web www.soundsscary.com

Tellington-TTouch (UK)
Gentle and innovative approach to care and training of animals.
Tel. 01761 471182
Web www.ttouchteam.co.uk

UK Registry of Canine Behaviourists
Professional body offering a referral service to vets and clients.
Tel. 01344 883955
Web www.ukrcb.org

INDEX

ACKNOWLEDGEMENTS

Thanks are due to Susanna Wadeson at Transworld and to Dr Hessayon; also to editorial and design team Brenda and Robert Updegraff and illustrator Claire Colvin, who have all been a pleasure to work with. Thanks to the team at Transworld: Deborah Adams, Lisa Gordon, Manpreet Grewal, Alison Martin and Gareth Pottle, and to Christine Shuttleworth for the index. Grateful acknowledgement is made to Gill Jackson and Angelina Gibbs for their painstaking proofreading. Thanks to Robin Watson for parasite illustrations on pages 112–113. Thanks to Sarah Wright at *Your Dog* magazine, to dog trainer extraordinaire Marie Miller for advice on training and behaviour, Tellington-Touch instructor Sarah Fisher for her constant inspiration and last but definitely not least, to all the dogs I have ever been privileged to own or meet and who have all contributed in some way to this book.

Photographs
Alamy: 4; 12 – bottom right; 15 – Hungarian Viszla, Lhasa Apso; 16 – Pekingese; 33 – top left; 44; 55 – top; 57; 60; 61; 70; 71; 73; 76; 77; 80 – left, right; 83; 91 – all; 97 – bottom; 98; 101; 102; 105; 108; 110; 111 – top; 115 – all; 121; 125.
iStock: 3; 10 – all; 11; 12 – top left, bottom left; 13 – Boston Terrier; 14 – Dobermann Pinscher, Setter, German Shepherd; 15 – Great Dane, Greyhound, Maltese; 16 – Newfoundland; 17 – Weimaraner; 19; 20; 21– top; 23; 25; 26; 28 – all except Pug; 30; 31; 32; 33 – top right, bottom right; 34; 35 – left; 36; 37; 39 – bottom; 40 – all; 41 – all; 45 – top right, bottom right; 49 – all; 52 – all; 53; 54 – all; 55 – bottom; 56 – all; 58 – left; 62; 63; 64; 65; 67; 69; 72; 74; 78; 79; 85; 92; 95 – all; 96 – all; 97 – top; 100; 103; 106; 107; 111 – bottom; 112; 114; 118; 122; 124.
Kennel Club: 99. **Transworld:** 38; 39 – top left, top right.
Warren Photographic: 5; 6; 7 – all; 8; 9; 12 – top right, middle right; 13 – all except Boston Terrier; 14 – Cocker Spaniel, Dachshund, Dalmation, Springer Spaniel, Golden Retriever; 15 – Jack Russell, Labrador Retriever, Schnauzer; 16 – all except Pekingese and Newfoundland; 17 – all except Weimaraner; 21 – bottom; 24; 28 – Pug; 35 – right; 58 – right; 59; 94; 109; 113.